CLOUD CAREER JOURNEYS

INSPIRING CHRONICLES OF INDIVIDUALS WHO HAVE CHOSEN THE "CLOUD PATH"

| Diverse Backgrounds | Unconventional Paths | Relentless Drive |

Text copyright © 2024 by Prasad Rao and Ashish Prajapati
All rights reserved.

No parts of this book may be reproduced without the written permission of the authors, except for the use of brief quotations in a book review.

For more information, contact the authors at
info@cloudcareerjourneys.com.

All individuals featured in this book have been contacted, and approval was secured before publishing their stories.

Self-published on Amazon and other platforms.

First Edition: 2024
Revision: 270124

Authors

Prasad Rao is a Principal Solutions Architect based out of UK focusing on modernizing legacy workloads to Cloud-native services. He leverages his experience to help customers build scalable architectures on Cloud. He also mentors diverse people to excel in their Cloud career journeys through his free mentoring initiative BeSA - Become a Solutions Architect.

Ashish Prajapati is a Technical Professional based out of UK. He is passionate about helping individuals and enterprises learn Cloud skills in an easy and fun way. He breaks down complex technical topic through unique analogies in his free mentoring initiative BeSA - Become a Solutions Architect. His work at www.analogiescloud.com is helping many Cloud enthusiasts get started with the Cloud, learn the fundamentals, and achieve Cloud certifications.

Editor

Poornima Menon is a Business Intelligence Engineer based out of UK and is also pursuing MBA in Data & Analytics. She is a voracious reader who manages to make her way through no less than 4 books a month, never tiring of discovering new authors and genres. With a keen eye for detail and a flair for weaving fresh perspectives into narratives, she couples her writing and communication skills with ingenuity.

Book Designer

Komal Telagavi, a Visual Designer and Book Illustrator, has transformed her childhood love for drawing into a fulfilling career. With a degree in architecture from NIT Trichy, she seamlessly integrates design principles into her work. Her work on projects like 'Tech Simplified' and 'Unshackled' has been exceptional. She helps craft beautiful designs, infusing illustrations, typography, color theory, and spatial awareness to create engaging visual experiences. She can be reached on LinkedIn @Komal-Telagavi.

Website Designer

Sunny is a freelance full-stack WordPress developer. With expertise in HTML, CSS, PHP, and JavaScript, he specializes in building high-performing landing pages, stunning personal sites, and robust websites on the WordPress platform. In addition, Sunny stays ahead of web design trends by continuously expanding his skills in platforms like Webflow, Wix, and Carrd. Sunny has a proven track record for delivering high-quality, functional websites on time and within budget. He can be reached at flawbecommunity@gmail.com.

Note from Authors

Issac Newton once wrote – "If I have seen further (than others), it is by standing on the shoulders of giants." If we look around, we will find circles of successful people around us, but most of the time, we don't know about the journey they have been through. What if there was a way to peek into the path they traveled, the turns they have taken, or the challenges they have overcome?

When it comes to career in Cloud computing, there is a ton of technical content, but aspirants are still confused about which path to take or how to excel in their Cloud career. We aim to address this gap by including different stories from people coming from diverse backgrounds and excelling in Cloud careers.

This book is an attempt to take you through the course of life they have been through, which shaped them the way they are today. After reading this book, you will feel as if you have met each of them individually and be inspired by them as we were when writing the book.

We are sure you will find bands of similarity and spectrums of difference in each journey; after all, if it was the exact same road to take to success, everyone could just have marched on, but it's not that simple. "Was it difficult for them? Will I face the same challenges? Will I be successful using the same methods?" These are real questions that may come to your mind, and let us tell you - we don't know the answers. But one thing we do know and assure you is that this book will help you learn about those journeys and will surely enlighten you to achieve your goals.

How to read this book?

The book covers the journey of 16 individuals that can each be read independently. Every journey has its own beginning and end. Feel free to read them sequentially or in any order that inspires you, or pick and read whichever story calls to you on any given day.

Every journey takes different twists and turns, but some commonality runs through each. We have arranged the book in six categories to reflect this and provide a structure. The idea is to ensure that the readers can resonate with at least one category based on their background, the career stage they are in, or their career aspirations. We meticulously selected every person in each category to ensure that we can present as unique and diverse Cloud career journeys as possible for you. You will also find AAA at the end of every story (more on this shortly).

When you flip through the book, you will find that we have used a hiking theme for the category illustration. Why hiking? Like hiking, building a Cloud career can range from a modest stroll to an epic journey, requiring varying levels of specialized skills and preparation. No matter where you are starting from in your Cloud career journey, the categories aim to motivate you to navigate your own unique career path forward.

The Pathfinders
Charted into Cloud with no technical background

> With resilience and grit, these intrepid explorers ventured into unfamiliar terrain to stake their claim in the lands of Cloud technology. Though their starting points differ, their stories inspire others to explore Cloud technology from any origin.

The Undefeated
Paved Cloud path against all odds

They regain the trail after detours and persist when the path gets tough. Though setbacks may force them to take a break or change course, these resilient explorers get back on their feet to find new paths to Cloud success.

The Progressives
Used prior IT knowledge as stepping stones to Cloud

With robust technical skills and determined ambition, these climbers conquered fresh trails to become lead guides in the Clouds. Their journeys show how foundational IT skills can pave upward paths to Cloud career peaks.

The Liberators
Eased the Cloud path for others

Through mentoring, teaching, and community building, they guide newcomers to bridge any gaps. By empowering those around them, they open new routes to the Cloud for all.

The Accelerators
Force multipliers for technology and Cloud explorers

They equip aspirants to soar in the Cloud and related technologies by elevating key competencies. They help multitude of followers in their rapid career progression through advocating and imparting crucial skills and knowledge.

The Pinnacles
At the apex of Cloud success

> They equip aspirants to soar in the Cloud and related technologies by elevating key competencies. They help multitude of followers in their rapid career progression through advocating and imparting crucial skills and knowledge.

What is AAA?

AAA stands for Advice, Action, and Alert from each of the individual featured in the book. They are:

- Top 3 **Advice** when following a Cloud career path
- Top 3 **Actions** to take that will drive meaningful progress
- Top 3 **Alerts** to avoid common pitfalls that can hinder success

The book shares 144 tips (16 stories x 9 tips) to advance your Cloud career. You may find overlapping tips across multiple stories. The more a tip is repeated across multiple stories, the more critical it is. Recurring tips signify the most important guidance for advancing your Cloud career.

What to do after reading the book?

Once you start reading the journeys featured in the book, you'll realize there is no single path to success. Every person follows a unique journey with challenges, failures, and lessons that shapes their path. There is no cookie-cutter approach to success. This book won't provide you with a step-by-step guide. It will encourage you to find your own path while showing you a guiding light.

We've included free resources from leading cloud training providers to support your cloud learning. The value of these free resources far outweighs the cost of this book. We've also created a separate digital product, Cloud Career Journeys - Starter Kit, to help advance your career.

Free Resources with the book

In the back pages of the book, you'll find a QR code to register and claim free resources. These include one-month free access to:

- Premium+ subscription to Whizlabs worth $29
- Premium subscription to Pluralsight Skills worth $45
- Digital Cloud Training's Learning Platform worth $19.99

Hopefully, these will help you to accelerate your Cloud career journey.

Cloud Career Journeys - Starter Kit

Based on feedback from our early readers, we have created the "Cloud Career Journeys - Starter Kit" to help readers advance their Cloud careers. The Starter Kit equips you with tools and resources to transform and advance your career within 6 to 12 months. It includes:

- Extended access to resources from leading Cloud training providers
- Step-by-step roadmaps to follow for various Cloud roles created by experts
- Access to exclusive community and monthly group sessions by experts on career guidance
- Discount Vouchers for professional resume-building services
- And more...

Please check the back pages for full details about what is included in the Cloud Career Journeys - Starter Kit. By following the roadmaps and utilizing the free learning resources, you should be able to achieve your Cloud career goals faster.

How to contact us?

The best way to connect with us is through LinkedIn, where we regularly share tips on excelling in your Cloud career. We also run a free mentoring program called BeSA (Become a Solutions Architect) along with other volunteers. You can find more details about this program at the end of the book.

Here are our LinkedIn socials:

Ashish Prajapati - https://www.linkedin.com/in/ash-tech/

Prasad Rao - https://www.linkedin.com/in/kprasadrao/

Journeys

The Pathfinders   1
Charted into Cloud with no technical background

01   **Daniel Gaina**   5
Senior Cloud Engineer,
AWS Community Builder

02   **Ifeanyichukwu Otuonye**   25
Cloud Engineer,
AWS Community Builder

03   **Eric Johnson**   45
Principal Developer Advocate,
AWS

The Undefeated   65
Paved Cloud path against all odds

04   **Jamila Jamilova**   69
Solutions Architect,
AWS

05   **Sandip Das**   91
Cloud Architect,
AWS Container Hero

06   **Parna Mehta**   111
Technical Trainer, AWS
AWS Authorized Instructor

| Journeys

The Progressives 135
Used prior IT knowledge as stepping stones to Cloud

07   Kesha Williams   139
Cloud & AI Leader,
AWS Machine Learning Hero

08   Sammy Cheung   159
AWS Ambassador,
Champion AWS Authorized Instructor

09   Lucy Wang   179
Founder,
Tech with Lucy

The Liberators 201
Eased the Cloud path for others

10   Jon Bonso   205
Co-Founder,
Tutorials Dojo

11   Neal Davis   227
Founder,
Digital Cloud Training

12   Julie Elkins   245
Senior Exam Prep Curriculum Developer,
AWS

Journeys

The Accelerators 267
Force multipliers for technology and Cloud explorers

13 **Nana Janashia** 271
    Founder,
    TechWorld with Nana

14 **Mumshad Mannambeth** 291
    Founder & CEO,
    KodeKloud

The Pinnacles 309
At the apex of Cloud success

15 **Ryan Kroonenburg** 313
    Founder,
    A Cloud Guru

16 **Jeff Barr** 335
    Vice President and Chief Evangelist,
    AWS

Start Your Journey

Free Resources 371
Starter Kit 381

The Pathfinders

Charted into Cloud with no technical background

With resilience and grit, these intrepid explorers ventured into unfamiliar terrain to stake their claim in the lands of Cloud technology. Though their starting points differ, their stories inspire others to explore Cloud technology from any origin.

The Pathfinders

The Pathfinders

Daniel Gaina
Senior Cloud Engineer,
AWS Community Builder

01 An Unconventional Beginning,
    A Thriving Cloud Career

Ifeanyichukwu Otuonye
Cloud Engineer,
AWS Community Builder

02 A Long Jump in Athletics,
    A High Jump Reaching Cloud

Eric Johnson
Principal Developer Advocate,
AWS

03 Once Preaching Sermons in Church,
    Now Advocating Cloud in Conferences

Pathfinders Undefeated Progressives Liberators Accelerators Pinnacles

An Unconventional Beginning, A Thriving Cloud Career

01

Daniel Gaina
Senior Cloud Engineer,
AWS Community Builder

Any journey worth admiration has one common element – discipline and if the journey is unconventional, it can be the most critical element required for success. Daniel's military school education has deep-rooted discipline, but he had to augment it with additional attributes for a career in the Cloud.

What else is needed for a successful Cloud career journey?

Daniel was born to working-class parents in Romania, whose grit and dedication to work, influenced his upbringing. Early in life, Daniel realized the value of hard work and is versatile in nature. Daniel attributes the first quality to his mother, a salesperson by profession, and the latter to his father, who had experience in doing multiple jobs.

"*I would not call myself a brilliant student while at school. I left home at the age of 14 to enroll in boarding – The Military High School. I initially wanted to join the Military Land Force Academy after graduating high school to become a sniper as I was good at shooting. But that was ruled out because I wore spectacles. I ended up at the Military Technical Academy, which also resonated more with my family's expectations.*"

This is an all-too-familiar tale of a young man finding himself in a stream that did not align with his aspirations, due to an obligation to keep his parents contented. He stayed enrolled in the military school for three years until he could not persevere any further. Daniel's stint at the formal university education ended in disqualification, for performing poorly in exams. However, the 7 years of education in the military academy, etched the seeds of self-discipline and self-confidence in his DNA.

"*I had no clue as to what I was going to do in life- All I knew was, I did not want to be a failure. Hence, I decided to chart my own course. At military school, we were told that (some would call it "propagandizing") "We" had the best shot of making it into the elite society, as we were studying at the finest military high school. This placed us in rare air. It gave us the idea that we could adapt to any environment by observing, learning, and just being confident.*"

With no formal university degree, looming confusion and immense uncertainty, Daniel was determined to travel abroad and explore a better career. This, combined with his knowledge of the English language, naturally gravitated him to find opportunities in the UK. Was a suitable opportunity waiting for him when he landed?

"*I didn't get off to a great start in the UK. Could not get a suitable job, so moved to Jersey, an island near France where I landed a job as a waiter. I was able to find this, exactly 4 days before running out of money and heading back to Romania. I think somehow destiny was on my side and helped me when I needed it the most. As this place was a seasonal high-end restaurant, I had to return to the UK after the season. I found another job in a pub in London and started there as a bartender.*"

His desire to be independent propelled him to face his new life head-on. His ambition and dedication made him quickly rise through the ranks and he became an Assistant Manager at the pub. Nevertheless, he realized that it was the end of the road for him as he would never be promoted to General Manager (he wasn't a British citizen). He found no further reason to cling on to that job any more.

"*I got a job at a taxi company-dispatching taxis as per customer requests on the night shift. I answered phone calls for 2 years during which time I started studying accounting, as I felt there seemed to be a gap in the market for Accountants. After studying on my own and passing 2 exams, I re-evaluated to realise that this was not something I wanted to do in the future. Later, I started to drive taxis as a freelancer for Uber and other companies. I had managed to save up a little and as I was not in a full-time job, I travelled through Europe and visited many countries. The one I enjoyed the most was when I traveled to Asia as a backpacker for 3 months.*"

When his taxi license was about to expire at the end of 2020, it catalyzed him to look for a career, not just odd jobs. By then he was 29 and knew it was about time he chose a stable career for a better future. He had set out four goals as requirements to choose his career path:

First: Should bring him financial stability

Second: Should *not* become obsolete in the future

Third: Should *not* require a university degree

Finally: Should let him work from anywhere

"*After a discussion with one of my friends, I realized that a job in IT seemed to perfectly fit the bill for all four goals and decided to give it a go. My friend, had a well-established IT career and encouraged me to explore several possibilities. He guided me through various IT profiles. In the end, I decided to take an entire year to study and prepare for a breakthrough into that field.*"

Some may call it too bold a move to give up existing sources of income, study for a whole year, and then look for an IT job, but not Daniel. Though he had no background in IT, his disciplined approach to various jobs, ever helpful friends, and a subtle aspiration to "make tomorrow better than today" gave him the confidence and motivation he needed to succeed. He left nothing to chance.

"*My military school education took over me. If I pour enough time into something, I will make it happen. I did not know when, I did not know how, nor did I know how long - All I knew was I would make it into IT. I did not expect any success instantly, but was ready to give it my best shot.*"

He did not consider himself a "smart kid," had not completed his university education, nor had any relevant experience. Yet, he was ready to face the challenges that he knew would come his way. His friend had encouraged him to explore Cloud technologies which attracted fresh talents, which had then (and even now!) seemed promising. Daniel was more drawn to the fact that it didn't require one to be a master of computers per se. Even professionals with years of experience were learning Cloud for the first time, so in a way it leveled the playing field.

"Due to the COVID lockdown, I moved back to Romania and stayed with my parents. For about a continuous 4 month time frame, I was confined to the four walls of my room and devoted all my time to studying the basics of Information Technology (I.T.). It was the first time I learned about what a 'network' was, or an IP address was and many more such things. As I was not earning and had very little to spend, I used my friend's Linux Academy platform subscription to learn and practice. The more I explored, the more I absorbed and enjoyed technology."

Ask Daniel what helped him most to grasp and remember all these new concepts, and he will tell you the learning mechanism – write it down (or type it down, even better!)

"I used to take handwritten notes. I think I had consumed over a thousand papers written because at the beginning of every term, every concept, every drawing was something new to me. I used to have a big stack of papers that helped me learn. But one day, I was looking for a particular topic. I searched for hours and hours, but in vain. That was when it dawned on me that it was time to go digital with my notes as I couldn't do a Ctrl F on my stack of papers, Can I?" Daniel chuckles.

After gathering all the details about the various career paths, Daniel focused on becoming a Solutions Architect. He chose this particular role because even though it is technical, it heavily involved customer interaction, which Daniel knew he enjoyed from his previous job experiences. Daniel always considered himself a people person, and he wanted to leverage that while trying to enter the Cloud roles.

He prepared for AWS Certified Solutions Architect - Associate certification by setting a tangible target. He chalked up a rigorous routine and started exploring all the terminologies and concepts mentioned in the exam guide. But, was that enough?

"I failed my first exam attempt. It was a reality check and that hurt. But I was determined not to go to the "easy Plan B - taxi driving job". The point is not to allow a setback to shatter our focus or detour to dictate our mindset. I was willing to sacrifice now, for the future. No matter what happens, no matter which job opportunity comes, I would not take any job other than a job in IT. This was my point of no return."

> *The point is not to allow a setback to shatter our focus or detours to dictate our mindset.*

Daniel recollected the story of Hernán Cortés, who had arrived on an island with 600 men and burned the ships upon arrival. This was an act that sent a clear message to Hernan's men that they had to - either conquer or die trying. Apparently, it took Cortés two years, but he succeeded.

Though, Daniel didn't pass the exam, his first attempt revealed his knowledge gaps. He bridged the gaps through focused preparation and more hands-on activities and two weeks later of his failed attempt, Aug 2020, he passed!

"*The success made me feel great. All my diligent study was now rewarded, but that is when I realized how important basics are. I have noticed, many community members suggest taking the AWS Certified Solutions Architect Associate certification directly. While that may hold true for experienced IT professionals, I'd say for someone like me, who is new to IT, it is better to first go for the AWS Certified Cloud Practitioner certification.*"

"*Then on, I figured that I must actively do more hands-on labs. I started completing lots of hands-on exercises, and that boosted my confidence. On a fine Sunday morning, at around 6 AM, I learned during a lab session, to send an SMS to my mobile- that was really cool! It is probably a very small thing, but to be able to witness how the theoretical concepts can be applied in a practical scenario was just mind blowing.*"

Passing the exam boosted Daniel's confidence, but he still needed a job. He didn't have the luxury to just keep on learning without worrying about having financial stability. He started leveraging LinkedIn to apply for jobs extensively while studying and passing the AWS Certified SysOps Associate certification. He continued studying through the Linux Academy platform and started using Whizlabs for practice exams.

"*Throughout September and October, I applied for about 300 to 400 jobs, but nothing materialized because of my lack of experience.*

> 💡 *I'd say for someone like me, who is new to IT, it is better to first go for the AWS Certified Cloud Practitioner certification.*

After many rejections, I finally got fortunate. I reached out to a LinkedIn influencer for help, and she kindly posted my profile to her followers. This amplification really helped. Sometimes it's not about "what" one knows but "who" one knows. The CEO of a Romanian security company reached out and offered me a job interview."

During the interview, Daniel emphasized his passion, willingness to learn, and his problem-solving attitude. He got hired as a Network Security consultant. That made him realize that showcasing other attributes can be more valuable in interviews than technical skills alone, especially for entry-level positions. When you have no technical expertise, you get hired for *all* that you bring to the table. His hunger for knowledge grew further. What's next?

"I wasn't complacent about this position. I believe that obtaining certifications opens doors, exhibits a positive attitude about learning new things, and proves one's grit. These certifications are particularly valuable for those without practical experience and demonstrate an employee's readiness for the job market. I completed my AWS Certified Developer Associate certification and continued to look for jobs in the AWS space."

Daniel continued to prioritize learning. He experimented extensively using the AWS Free Tier account and completed tons of hands-on labs. He dedicated his spare time to further study AWS and pursued additional certifications to solidify his base, such as

> 💡 Sometimes it's not about "what" one knows but "who" one knows.

CompTIA Network+ and CompTIA Security+. All those times, he stuck to learning like paper clips to magnets. He also kept on expanding his LinkedIn network during the period. He purposely started connecting with people in different Cloud-based roles.

"I actively started networking with Cloud Engineers, Solutions Architects, and other Cloud-based profiles. I compared my CV with people who were in those roles and started looking for the skills I missed. And when I found certain skills that were mentioned in multiple profiles, I started learning about those skills and technologies too."

Daniel came across a person on LinkedIn who was referring candidates for jobs at AWS Ireland. When he reached out to her, she asked if he wanted to be recommended for a Cloud Support Engineer position. There was nothing to lose, so he gave it a try. To his utter surprise, AWS responded and invited him for a technical interview. It was a validating moment that confirmed he was on the right track. He was ready to take the chance.

"At that time, I did not know how to prepare for the interview. I was 100% sure that I was not ready for this. I underwent a technical assessment but did not make it to the next round. Nevertheless, the fact that AWS considered me with less than a year of experience, no IT background, and no formal graduation - boosted my confidence. It was March 2021 and I knew that even if it wasn't happening now,

> 💡 *I compared my CV with people who were in those roles and started looking for the skills I missed.*

doesn't mean that it wouldn't in the future. I will wait for that time and be ready for it when it comes my way again."

Through LinkedIn, he transitioned as a Cloud Support Engineer in another Romanian company, focusing on OpenStack. Although it wasn't AWS, it still had *cloud* in the position title. Daniel took it as a chance to continue learning and gain valuable experience with Linux and on-premise services.

"*I started my second IT job in May 2021 and embarked on a learning curve, diving deep into Linux, shell scripting, and various OpenStack services. It was not AWS-specific, but I was still learning useful things that I thought would be useful in the future. I figured that if I could make it through then, I would be able to understand the underlying technologies better.*"

Daniel kept expanding his spectrum of knowledge. He had all 3 associate-level certifications and a few CompTIA certifications. He was certain that the knowledge he gained while pursuing these certifications would help him in the future. Another thing to note was that, he was not treating it as a *tick-in-the-box* activity. His third job opportunity arose when he saw a Facebook ad for a remote AWS Engineer position for a Lithuanian company.

"*Despite my initial hesitance about proceeding with the job application on Facebook, I went ahead and applied to later discover that it was a role with an AWS Partner company based in Lithuania. The allure of remote work prompted me to accept the position. Eventually, I relocated to London while remotely working for this company. Finally, I was going to work on AWS technologies.*"

Daniel had reached a certain point in IT career and started working as an AWS Engineer, but he ensured this success didn't get in his head. It was like the *playing ground* had changed. If earlier you were playing poker at a family gathering, now it was like playing professionally at a club!

"*I decided that I was going to get stronger from a technical point of view and also became sharply focused on AWS. I knew that I would be working with people who would have way more experience than me in IT. Some may also be the ones who has written zillion lines of code, or even the ones who helped Netflix to deploy their streaming architecture for millions of viewers. But, I wanted to be the go-to AWS guy. There wasn't going to be an AWS-related question for which I might not know the answer or at least have a way to figure out the answer.! I knew there was no shortcut. The harder I work, the better I get, the higher I get.*"

Juggling between his day job and continuous learning was demanding and requiring significant sacrifices. He was working hard to gain as much experience as possible to become a Senior Engineer as quickly as possible. In the preparation, Daniel started setting targets, reasonable expectations and a tangible objective and pursued it relentlessly. He knew he was not running a sprint, he was running a marathon- an incredibly fast one. He wanted to be in the elite line-up.

"*Currently, I work as a consultant for an AWS Partner company. My day-to-day responsibilities revolve around helping other companies harness the full power of AWS services. This entails integrating new services into their existing workloads, configuring* their setups correctly, optimizing costs, and conducting security assessments. My team and I aim to be experts on the AWS platform, guiding customers so they can make the most out of its capabilities."

"My focus and passion lie in the world of technology. It's not just a job for me; it's something that I genuinely enjoy and take pleasure in. I find myself constantly learning and exploring new things related to my field. Even in my free time, I immerse myself in topics like AI and other interesting technical subjects. It's not about impressing my boss or meeting work-related goals, it's about personal fulfilment."

Looking back, Daniel thinks he has successfully achieved the four goals he initially set for his IT career. He currently enjoys the freedom of working remotely and has achieved financial stability. The ever-evolving nature of the tech industry keeps him on his toes and fulfilled, and he finds himself being of value to both society and himself.

* * *

Daniel's plans include further refining his technical skills and gaining hands-on experience in customer engagements and projects. He continues to achieve more AWS certifications – AWS Certified Security Speciality Certification, AWS Certified Database Speciality Certification and recently passed the challenging AWS Certified Solutions Architect Professional Certification as well! He aspires to obtain all AWS certifications one day.

Furthermore, he is preparing to become an AAI, or Amazon

Authorized Instructor[1] where he plans to deliver AWS trainings and teach others how to utilize AWS services in the best way possible.

Along with all of this, Daniel also wants to contribute back to the community as much as he can. He helps people on LinkedIn and Discord by sharing his learning. In March 2023, he became an AWS Community Builder[2] and started his YouTube channel - Daniel Talks Tech[3], wherein he rightly calls himself a self-made AWS Engineer with no IT background and without attending any IT bootcamp. He aims to present new IT professionals with a roadmap to break into the Cloud through his channel.

Daniel's success story is one that germinated from the turmoil, and it ingrained in him qualities like discipline, perseverance, hard work, determination, and self-confidence. His journey is all about *"making tomorrow better than today"*.

---

[1] https://aws.amazon.com/training/aai/

[2] https://aws.amazon.com/developer/community/community-builders/

[3] https://www.youtube.com/@danieltalkstech22/

ADVICE

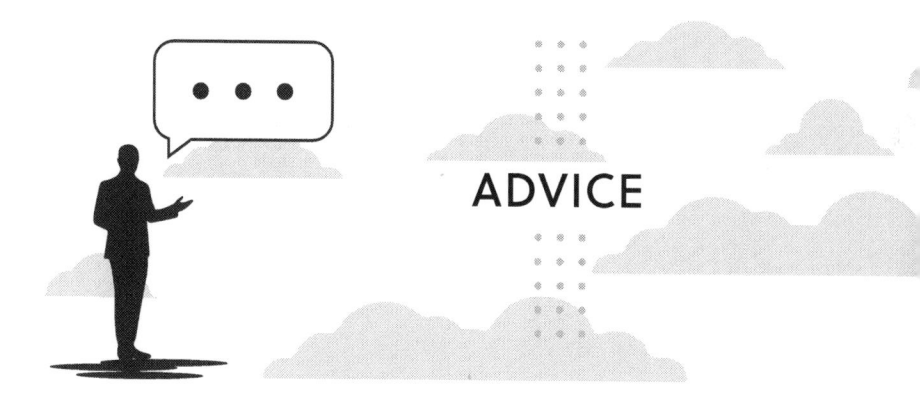

Advice when following a Cloud career path

- **Prepare for a marathon, not a sprint** - Your career journey is a marathon; you will need endurance and a long-term plan. Don't get disappointed by setbacks, and don't be complacent after success.

- **Widen your knowledge search** - Don't restrict yourself to one learning platform. Explore various learning platforms and style of learning.

- **Build your network** - Connect with people who are already in the role you aspire to be in. Understand their skills and knowledge and strive to attain a similar level.

ACTION

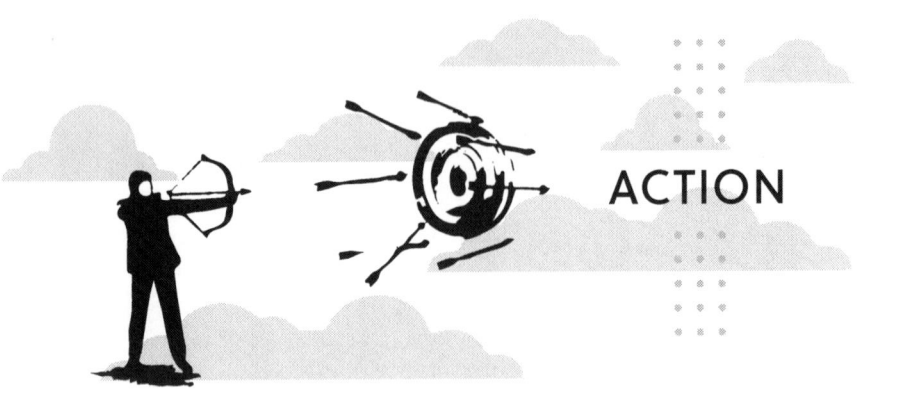

Actions to take that will drive meaningful progress

- **Set tangible targets** - Write them down and map out the steps you need to take to reach that target. It could be a job role, a certification, or mastering a technology.

- **Document your learning journey** - Share it on platforms like LinkedIn, Medium, or YouTube. This not only helps reinforce your learning, but also showcases your progress and expertise to others. Remember, the more you articulate your journey, the more confident you become.

- **Practice what you learn** - Apply the knowledge you have just gained, and figure out a way to see it in action. This will help you retain that knowledge for a long time and boost your confidence.

ALERT

Alerts to avoid common pitfalls that can hinder success

- **Avoid being shy about asking for help** - There is a wide world out there ready to help you. One must be brave enough to ask for help when needed, regardless of the hesitation, ego, or position.

- **Stay away from shortcuts** - You may be able to pass a certification by learning the answers, but then you are cheating yourself and no one else. Learn for yourself, not for someone else.

- **Don't be complacent** - Technology evolves at fast pace, so don't be left behind. If you are not moving forward, it means you already started moving backward.

Pathfinders | Undefeated | Progressives | Liberators | Accelerators | Pinnacles

A Long Jump in Athletics, A High Jump Reaching Cloud

02

Ifeanyichukwu Otuonye

Cloud Engineer,
AWS Community Builder

A pro athlete needs stamina, speed, strength, skill and spirit. Ifeanyi had it all. He was channeling these five S's to get closer to another S - Success. But will it be the same for his Cloud career journey too?

Were the life lessons learned On the Track enough to transition to Cloud technology?

B orn to Nigerian parents, Ifeanyi was the middle child and the most adventurous one in the family of three boys. His name means 'nothing is impossible with God.' Drawing power from his name, he started to defy the odds from a young age. When he was four years old, his parents migrated from Nigeria to the Turks and Caicos Islands in the Caribbean. Ifeanyi learned early in life from his father that you can achieve anything through hard work and dedication.

"*My father was a lawyer with almost a decade of experience in Nigeria. But he had to restart his career as an entry-level lawyer in the islands. His dedication and perseverance got him promoted every year and he became the Deputy Attorney General of Turks and Caicos Islands and proceeded to hold even higher prestigious government roles. My parents had well established the importance of education right from the early days of schooling."*

Ifeanyi outshined their expectations by being a top performer throughout his primary and high school education. But as he was a more energetic person he could not contain his vitality only to his studies and therefore inched towards Parkour and Free Running, which was then a big thing. As Ifeanyi had no coaches to help him with structured training, he learned from his natural abilities.

His life-altering moment came at the age of 15, when he won a silver medal for his county in a high jump at an international competition. There was no looking back as he realized there were endless possibilities and opportunities before him. There was a world beyond the ocean, and he was ready to conquer it.

"It was then I learned that there is so much more outside the Caribbean. I had a lot of potential in me and I realized that it is not impossible to aspire for bigger dreams. Limited resources don't limit me as a person, and there is still so much for me to tap into the world."

Ifeanyi's initial strides to success did not go unnoticed. A Jamaican coach was impressed by his performance even with no formal training. He offered him a 2-year focused program in *Track and Field* to train among the best. In the pursuit of excellence at the age of 15, Ifeanyi left for Jamaica. While in his second year there, Vincent Johnson, an athletic college recruiter from the United States, discovered his performance.

Like a magnet attracting iron particles, Ifeanyi was attracting opportunities in his life. He was given a chance to move to the United States of America in order to pursue college education and also compete for the *Track and Field* team of Kansas State University with a full student scholarship. He was willing to get cuts in order to be a diamond.

"*I was blown away to know that they were fully paying for my college education so I could be a part of their athletic team and run for the university. I didn't think something like this was possible. It was a life-changing opportunity for me, and I ended up accepting it. I enrolled at Kansas State University to pursue a Bachelor's Degree in Electrical Engineering. Simultaneously, I also started to rigorously train in the University's sports team.*"

This led to Ifeanyi having a tough schedule, which impacted his academic grades. He scored a mere 1.6 GPA in his first semester of Electrical Engineering. That is when he started questioning his abilities for the first time in his life. When failure smothers you, it shuts out all light and leaves you with nothing to cling on to for any hope. The playing field has completely changed. Can he overcome this hurdle?

"*I was depressed for few days. I figured that the American education system was very different from what I was used to. I also realized that Electrical Engineering was not for me. Being an*

> *I was familiar with losses and wins. Also, standing back up, taking chances, and trying again was not new to me.*

athlete, I was familiar with losses and wins. Also, standing back up, taking chances, and trying again was not new to me. Hence, the next semester I changed my major and got myself into Information Systems (IT). This time, I ended up graduating with a 3.3 GPA. I knew that this change in my major was going to change my life for the better."

As a *checkmark* provides athletes with a visual cue on the runway indicating the start of their approach, Ifeanyi spotted his *checkmark* for his IT journey to begin his run-up.

By the time Ifeanyi graduated, his athletic career had skyrocketed. He became one of the world's Top 30 Pro Athletes, which landed him a deal with Nike. Kansas State University decided to pay for his Master's degree, which was a huge blessing. It allowed Ifeanyi to go straight from a Bachelor's to a Master's at the same university and he could continue to use their resources and coaches to train and compete. *Track and Field* athletes are given much lesser contracts compared to other sports, so Nike's contract wasn't enough to cover all his expenses. To support himself while studying, Ifeanyi worked as an IT Support for his college's sports organization.

"There were many challenges that I used to face in my job in the beginning as an IT Support Engineer, but my managers and co-workers would help me overcome all those difficulties. When I started, I did not know how to run a CLI script on a Windows or a Linux server. I was a bit ashamed because I should have known it as an Information Systems graduate. But what helped me most was communicating things that I did not know to my manager. So, he started helping me with small tasks initially, and soon enough, I was *intricate in managing dedicated servers. I was enjoying every bit of learning, slowly gaining the pace."*

This job was Ifeanyi's first real-life exposure to the field of technology. He started getting a taste of the IT industry as a young professional. But sometimes, life hatches unexpected turns, and soon you realize that you can't steer away from it. After his Masters, he got a job as a Technical Sales Representative that he absolutely loved. He welcomed that job and felt his career was taking off, but US immigration laws ended his stint in the country. His then company filed for his H1B visa, so he could continue employment with them but at that time there was a high decline rate. His visa application was declined, and he had to leave the US. He faced an abrupt and unplanned departure from the U.S., clipping his time there short - like a long jumper whose flight phase ends sooner than expected.

The superstar sportsperson with a Master's degree returned to Turks and Caicos. He had seen the most significant events in the world of sports and was offered a Sports Event Manager job to bring international sports events experience to Turks and Caicos national sports. While on this job, he soon realized that he did not have the extensive event management experience needed, hence it was a steep learning curve for him. Ifeanyi was still training as an athlete, and managing sports events along with it was very stressful.

He got married three months after joining this new job. Ifeanyi

But what helped me most was communicating things that I did not know to my manager.

was finding it hard to spend quality time with his better half because of his hectic schedule in his current job.

"*I was always overworked, and it was overwhelming. I was bringing some of my work stress home, which was not good. So, I thought I needed to choose a career that I would enjoy, that gives me flexibility, has a clear growth path, and pays me well so I can provide a better life for my family. I had decided to enter IT again because I was very passionate about it and I used to enjoy working in IT Support. However, this field is so vast that I was unsure which path I should take. I started from the basics until I chanced upon the technology - The Cloud.*"

He started building a steady foundation for his IT marathon by acquiring the CompTIA A+, Network+, and Security+ certifications. It was his *Ancillary training* before specializing further, just as a distance runner might lift weights to build overall strength for the long haul ahead. He shored up his core knowledge base, just like an athlete prepares their body.

He knew that these certifications would build a strong foundation for him in IT. He was building the momentum to take the high jump. Ifeanyi did his thorough research on Cloud technologies and different Cloud providers. He felt it was the next big thing, and he needed to double down on learning the technology of one of the major Cloud providers.

"*My main goal was to learn AWS as they are the pioneers and biggest Cloud providers, but I began with Azure and appeared for the Azure Fundamentals Certification. My thought process was that, after I secured the beginner Azure certification, I would be able to channelize my entire attention and focus onto AWS and eventually have a good exposure to both of them. But nothing went ahead as planned. I failed my Azure Fundamentals certification. I had studied very hard and thought I had it in my bag, but it completely knocked me off. I questioned myself whether I was doing the right thing by going down this path as I could not even clear the fundamental exam. The failure was my truth serum."*

No, this *cannot* be the end of his Cloud career journey! And that's where a sportsperson's spirit triumphs. Sportspersons train for years for important sports events. And if they cannot perform on that day, for that split second, does that mean they should pack their bags forever? Are there no more laps? He leaned out to his learning from the sports world.

"As a sportsperson, you fail quite frequently, and you learn the ability to bounce back. I was a long jumper and trained for World championships for 2 years. The entire Turks and Caicos was rooting for me. In a long jump event, you get three attempts. I remember in the 2015 IAAF World Championships; my first attempt was fouled as I stepped overboard. Second attempt – fouled. And on the third attempt – fouled again. I failed to record even a valid jump."

"It felt like I had let my country down and wasted my time. But you know that's not true. All the training hours you have accumulated

> 💡 All the training hours you have accumulated are not wasted.

are not wasted. I continued training hard, and two years later, I went to the Commonwealth Games and broke the national record."

Ifeanyi holds the current National record[1] for the Turks and Caicos Islands in the Long Jump.

His bruised pride was hungry for a payback after his failed certification attempt. With that innate spirit, one can imagine that passing an Azure certification after failing the first attempt will not be difficult for a national record holder. With the Azure fundamentals certification baton in his hand, he was charged up to give his all to learn AWS. He started learning AWS and achieved AWS Certified

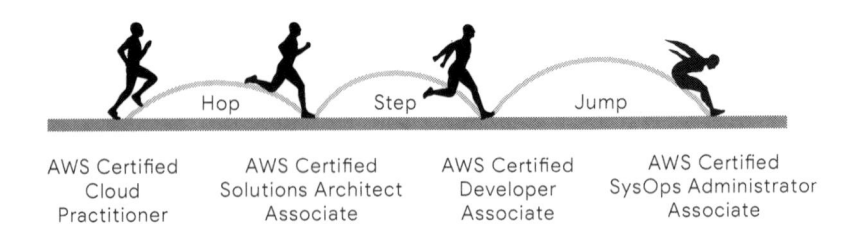

Hop	Step	Jump	
AWS Certified Cloud Practitioner	AWS Certified Solutions Architect Associate	AWS Certified Developer Associate	AWS Certified SysOps Administrator Associate

Cloud Practitioner Certification (CCP).

Like an approach run provides a gradual acceleration to the athlete before the jump, Ifeanyi's certification gave him required momentum for the career leap. Then, swiftly clearing the next three hurdles - AWS Certified Solutions Architect Associate, AWS Certified Developer Associate, and AWS Certified SysOps Administrator Associate certifications - his progress resembled a triple jump. Sequencing certifications strategically, he stepped stone to stone,

---

[1]https://en.wikipedia.org/wiki/Ifeanyichukwu_Otuonye

steadily broadening his IT and Cloud knowledge, just as a triple jumper builds through each phase from hop to step to jump.

Ask him why he was focusing on getting all these certifications, and he would explain how certifications helped him gradually learn IT and the Cloud.

"*For someone who does not have a lot of IT background, certifications provide the much-needed structured learning path. After Azure fundamentals, and as I already had CompTIA certifications, I was tempted to go for AWS SA Associate certification directly. However, I went for AWS CCP, which provides a broad understanding of all the AWS services at a high level, which is essential before diving deep into those services in SA Associate. Also, for Associate-level certifications, I deliberately went for SA associate first, then for the Developer, and then for SysOps. Some say developer certification is easy but it was tough for me as I am not from a developer background.*"

Ifeanyi was still working as a full-time Sports Event Manager and simultaneously pursuing his goal to enter Cloud Engineering by clearing the initial certifications. He used three primary resources for all these certifications - Stephane Maarek courses on Udemy, Neil Davis practice tests on Udemy, and Tutorial Dojo practice tests. He also honed his expertise through a lot of hands-on labs. He devised his own methodology to learn AWS and got AWS Certified, which worked well for him. To his surprise, he later became the first Cloud Engineer in Turks and Caicos. He is a national record holder and the first Cloud Engineer on the island. What could have held him back now?

"*I reached out to one of the most technologically advanced companies in the Turks and Caicos and explored for an opportunity to exercise my Cloud skills. They said that they plan to move to the Cloud after 5 years or so. At that moment, I knew I would have to search globally for job opportunities. It was the same as after winning a silver medal at 15. I had to go abroad for better training. I was in a similar situation again. After all the Cloud certifications I achieved, I had to search for international jobs as opportunities were very limited on the island.*"

Ifeanyi had to find a new *sandpit* - an area in a jumping event where the athlete lands. He started applying for jobs abroad. He thought that, as he had all these certifications it should suffice to secure a job easily, but he was not getting any interview calls, mainly because he lacked real-life hands-on experience. What then helped him land a job? A 6-month bootcamp, Level Up In Tech, founded by an individual who himself transitioned from banking to the Cloud industry. The bootcamp provides a strategic learning path that focuses on real-world experience.

"*The Bootcamp helped me with three things. First, I worked on complex projects, which I would not have been able to do by myself. Second, it encouraged us to learn in public, and that played a pivotal role for me in securing a job. Third, it helped us improve our communication and collaboration. It's not just about understanding the technology but also about explaining it in a simplified manner to others.*"

Sportspersons are used to performing in front of the public all their life. They don't get distracted by the audience. In fact, it gives them the required motivation, and they know how the crowd-cheering can get the best out of them. That is why, learning in public resonated well with Ifeanyi.

"*I went on to LinkedIn and started posting all the work I did in those six months of bootcamp. Starting from Linux to AWS to Python and then Docker, Kubernetes, and Terraform. Soon enough, other experienced Cloud Engineers started helping me. They were giving me feedback and appreciating my work from time to time. What also surprised me was that many people reached out to seek my mentorship.*"

He was at the start of his journey but soon realized that someone always benefits from the learnings you share. He started helping people as much as he could, but he did not have the luxury of unlimited bandwidth to mentor all the people. He started posting about the resources others can use to learn and upskill themselves. Ifeanyi's willingness to actively interact with others by sharing knowledge and technical insights to help others helped him to become an AWS Community Builder[1].

"*During my journey to become a Cloud Engineer, one of my dreams for my career was to work at AWS. As I researched the company, I stumbled on the many different communities, events, and affiliations. That's how I found out about the AWS Community Builders program and the vast amount of benefits that come with it if accepted into the program.*"

The AWS community builder program offers technical resources,

---

[1] https://aws.amazon.com/developer/community/community-builders/

education, and networking opportunities to AWS technical enthusiasts and emerging thought leaders who are passionate about sharing knowledge and connecting with the technical community.

"*This passion for helping others got me hired as an AWS instructor in the same bootcamp after I completed the course. I designed and developed course material introducing Cloud computing concepts and AWS services to students from diverse backgrounds, empowering them in the first 4 weeks towards passing the AWS Certified Cloud Practitioner exam. For the short 3 months I worked at the bootcamp, coached/mentored over 70 students, and helped over 50 pass the certification.*"

Having an active online presence helps you in more ways than expected. You never know who you're inspiring. Potential employers had started noticing Ifeanyi's work. His informative and engaging posts spoke for themselves as he continued to share his learning and help others in the community. He did not have to apply for jobs and wait for them to call back anymore. People were reaching out to him

I followed this approach to learn about cloud.

He is diligent. Let's hire him.

I will use the same resources.

I will follow the same approach.

proactively to know more about his work.

"The CEO of the Security Blue Team asked me to join their Cloud Engineering team in London. They had reviewed my work from what I had done in the bootcamp, which I had shared online, and were eager to make me a part of their organization. I had to go through two rounds of interviews which were focused more on behavioural as they had already inspected my work through my online presence. Within a week, I was presented with the job offer letter. This was such a novel experience for me as I never saw it coming. But it was something that I had worked hard for and was preparing myself for these past few years. I accepted their offer and became a full-time Cloud Engineer for the Security Blue Team."

It is not difficult to draw parallels between his athletics journey and Cloud career journey. The hard work of multiple years finally culminates in the glory point. He applied all the life learning from his tracks to ensure he succeeded in the Cloud.

"Becoming a Cloud Engineer to me was pivoting my life's journey from tracks to technology. I started noticing this undying passion that I had for information technology, and I just could not let it slide away. I knew there would be many hurdles on the way and it would not be an easy win, but I was ready to make these changes in my life for a better future ahead."

> The hard work of multiple years finally culminates in the glory point.

So, what are Ifeanyi's plans for the future, then? For now, a continuous learning journey but with a clear goal to work for AWS in the near future.

"*Someday in the future, I wish to work in AWS as it was the anchor that held me throughout my journey so far. Going forward, I would like to see myself specializing in one of the Cloud services and building my career around it, but currently, I'm eager to work in the diverse aspects of the Cloud as a certified Cloud Engineer and to help others.*"

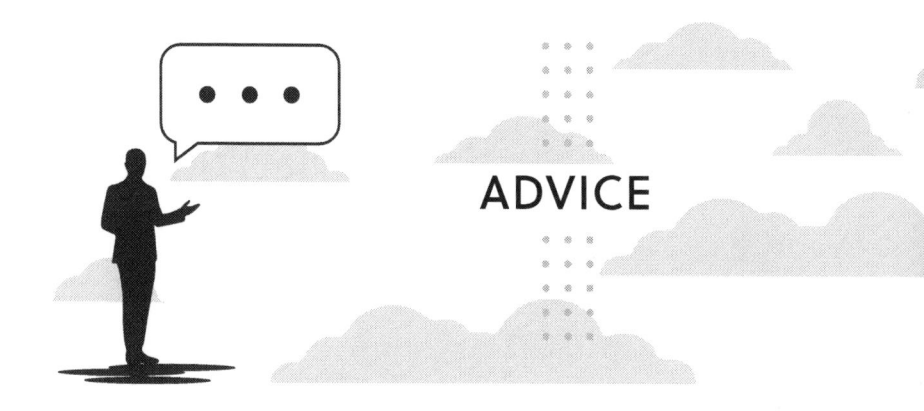

Advice when following a Cloud career path

- **Don't be scared to dream big** - whatever seems impossible for somebody else doesn't necessarily have to be impossible for you.

- **Find your passion** - And then pursue it relentlessly with grit and persistence. Remember that you may not find your passions in a single day.

- **Start, don't wait** - It's a journey, so focus on progression, not perfection.

ACTION

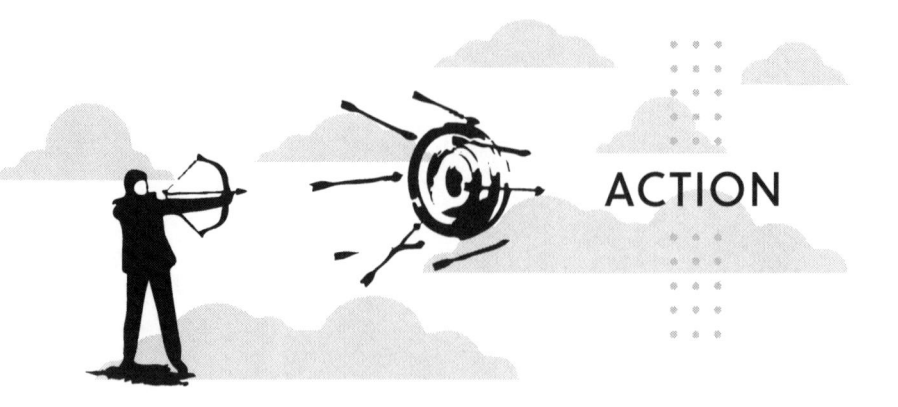

Actions to take that will drive meaningful progress

- **Do as many hands-on labs as possible** - try to work on complex real-life projects.

- **Learn and build in public** - you'd be surprised with the support the community provides.

- **Share your learnings with others** - if you can explain to others, it means you have actually understood the concepts.

ALERT

Alerts to avoid common pitfalls that can hinder success

- **Don't try to learn too many things simultaneously** - Technology is vast, so try and narrow it down to specific things you want to learn.

- **Thinking that you will get a job as soon as you pass certification** - getting certified and getting a job are not the same.

- **Letting self-doubt overpower you** - Especially when you hit a roadblock like failing a certification and not getting a job interview.

Pathfinders Undefeated Progressives Liberators Accelerators Pinnacles

Once Preaching Sermons in Church, Now Advocating Cloud in Conferences

03

Eric Johnson

Principal Developer Advocate,
AWS

Faith and reason are regarded as two means by which an understanding and knowledge of God may be gained and maintained. Sometimes these two are complementary; other times they are in contradiction. Eric knew this well while studying theology and becoming a young pastor.

Did he lean on these means again, while becoming a cloud evangelist?

Tucked away in the well-known high temperature of Phoenix, Arizona, Eric's home was a pleasant abode. The rising mercury of the outside had no effect on the cozy and loving oasis of his home. Like his brother, Eric was born with a condition called Monodactyl which means that he only has a single finger on each of his hands and only one toe on each of his feet.

In Eric's household, faith and family are considered above everything else. Their family would be at church every Sunday morning and Wednesday night. From the early age of life, he was taught to believe that everything happens according to the almighty's God's plan.

"*My father was a biology teacher in a public school for 45 years and even worked as a consultant for private and charter schools. And* as I grew older, my mother became the Minister of Music for our local church. Both my parents were passionate about their respective professions."

Though their vocations did not yield riches, his parents worked under their faith in God to provide their children with a comfortable life. They were not awash in wealth, but provided a warm nest for their children to grow and thrive. What their bank accounts lacked, their hearts made up for tenfold.

"My father was always our biggest cheerleader and protector. One day while shopping in a Home Depot Store, my father thought that some fellow shopper had purposely insulted my older brother with regards to his hands. Without a second thought he punched the other man."

Though not prone to violence, Eric's father would turn the world on its head with the force of a typhoon to safeguard his loved ones from harm. So, when he felt his son was insulted, he struck with all the protective fury. He was no brawler, but his devotion was unbending as stone and he would shake the heavens to keep his beloved family from hurt. And that has taught young Eric an important lesson of his life – *always protect the family.*

Eric's mother on the other hand was the heart of their home, her love as warm and constant as the sun. She was the guiding compass, teaching her children how to navigate daily activities with grace. As she was born with the same condition of Monodactyl, she ensured her children confronted each challenge head-on, never exploiting their situation for personal gain.

> "One of my friends in grade school, who just stood 35 inches tall had convinced our English teacher that writing hurt his hands and got exempted from half the homework assignments. Based on his advice I also falsely claimed in the school that writing caused my hand to pain and the teacher gave me the same concession. But when my mom uncovered our mischief, she marched me right back to school and revealed my dishonesty to the teacher. Mom even went to Mark's house and notified his parents about the trickery we cooked up together."

This experience proved to be a formative one for Eric, imparting lessons he would carry throughout his life. He learned not to expect special treatment because of his condition, as doing so would only invite others to define him by his differences.

The incident shaped Eric's moral compass, guiding him to meet life's challenges on his own merits and not the concessions owed to hardship. The deception had taught him more than any homework assignment could about what it means to live with honesty, ethics and stand tall as one's true self in the world.

Growing up, Eric had started to play soccer and his dad coached him to improve, but his true passion was drumming. Even as a goalie on the soccer pitch, rhythms pulsed through Eric's mind. His love for the drums only grew stronger, hence he wanted to learn it. But, how

> 💡 He learned not to expect special treatment because of his condition, as doing so would only invite others to define him by his differences.

can he hold a drumstick with only one finger in each of his hands?

"My passion for drumming was growing immensely. A lot of people had told me that I couldn't achieve this goal because of my hands. But I saw that as a challenge. And also, I had a supportive father who would come up with unique ideas on how I could hold the drumsticks. The one idea that finally worked was when I put the drumsticks in my wristbands and used hair ties to adjust the grip."

Eric's enthusiasm for playing the drums was so intense that he attended community college to formally learn drumming, believing his skills were solid. Hungry to advance, he later went to the School of Music at Grand Canyon University. But the other drummers at the music school were far more skilled and next to them, Eric's performance was rudimentary. Was he failing to pursue his passion?

While in the music school, Eric got romantically involved and got married. His wife was then attending nursing school at the same University. Paying for both their degrees proved difficult. Eric's struggle to excel at the school got aggregated with the financial crunch of their fees, which made him drop out of music school. He began working full-time so his wife could finish her program and become a nurse. Just as he learned from his father, Family *always* comes first.

"As I mentioned, faith has always been a huge part of my family and my life. Right after abandoning my music degree, I started working in Ministry at our Church. For me, this job felt like a calling from God. Soon, I went back to college again earned a bachelor's degree in Creative Arts of Worship – Theology. But, it took me nine

years instead of the actual 4 years to finally settle on a degree because I have had to start it all over again."

After earning his bachelor's degree, Eric worked as a youth pastor, preaching about faith and life in Phoenix for about three years. Through this, he discovered an honest passion for motivational speaking which eventually became his second calling. Some years later, he moved to Texas to pursue a Master's degree in Divinity from a seminary in Texas. But God had his plans for Eric.

Up until this point, everything he knew about computers came from self-directed online learning. He had no formal IT training, but an enduring drive to understand technology. Eric got his chance when he worked in the seminary's IT department for a year as a Microsoft Exchange Administrator. He later spent 2 years assisting with Web and Media Development, toggling between the roles. Though new to the field, Eric pursued IT with enthusiasm, faith and reason. Was he now attaining the much-needed enlightenment?

"I took a few basic computer courses alongside my masters and then enrolled myself in a Java class. It was a bold move to take a programming language class without any prior coding background. Not surprisingly, it did not work out in my favor. Just two weeks after starting Java, I had to drop out of the course."

Despaired by his decisions, Eric moved back to Phoenix to work as an associate pastor only to shift back to Texas after a couple of months to continue his Masters. Like a leaf blown about in the wind, he was confused and overworked, unsure of his true path.

Over three turbulent years in the early 2000s, Eric was tossed between states. His life was a stormy sea that eventually, affected his marriage and ended up in divorce. After separating from his wife, he followed her to eastern Colorado to co-parent their three sons. He tended to his fatherly duties but was adrift, seeking a new horizon. Eric had stepped down from being a pastor and even dropped out of his master's degree. His life was a tangled knot that he desperately needed to untie and reorder. But as one door closed, a gate to opportunity in IT swung open.

"I had started looking for jobs. Finally, in the October of 2006 I landed a job as a designer for an Online Event Registration Company. At this company, I was responsible for designing their marketing website. I have to admit that a lot of my designs were repetitive. But I was working with grit and contributed significantly to building websites."

"Coincidently, the only Developer in our department quit his job. And our company started looking for another one. I was on a vacation for two weeks while this episode unfolded and when I resumed back at work, I learned that they had hired another designer, which was actually my position at the company. I thought I had lost my job but to my astonishment, I ended up wearing a C# developer hat. They trusted my skills and were willing to give me a chance. I did not see that coming, but it was a great opportunity."

The dark clouds were lifting. Eric's days of drifting aimlessly were subsiding. The winds of change had steered him off course but also brought him to the shores of a new beginning. Eric was now working as a developer. He had done some work on HTML and JavaScript in his previous job at the seminary but this was his first opportunity to work as a professional developer full-time.

"At this new position I did not have the best knowledge of the work I was doing but I used to surf through search engines frequently to have a better understanding. I knew how everything was conceptually possible but I just didn't know the syntax for it. So, I made Google my best friend and found all my answers from it."

By this time, the storm in his personal life that started during his divorce had calmed down. He remarried and had two daughters, settling into a newfound stability. Meanwhile at work, the company that Eric worked for went through a few different sales and acquisitions. Eric's role nurtured steady growth because of his passion for technology. He was soon promoted to a Senior Developer role.

Eric's employers also began adopting cloud services, selecting AWS as their preferred cloud vendor. The rapid and steady pace of innovation at AWS was the key factor in their selection. Cloud was becoming a new school of thought for him.

"Cloud had simultaneously enchanted and piqued my curiosity. Soon I was ramping up on Cloud Technologies. When I find something interesting, I sink my teeth into it and try to learn every single aspect of it. So, I started building projects in AWS. This hands-on experience helped me in understanding the technology better."

> Eric's role nurtured steady growth because of his passion for technology.

Eric soon started to see beyond the code, like Neo (played by Keanu Rives) understood "The Matrix". His focus turned toward designing solutions rather than just compiling a program. As his expertise started growing, he started looking for opportunities to feed the "architect" in him. What was he going to build next?

In 2014, he joined a start-up called Showpitch as a Senior Software Architect. There, he worked closely with their hosting provider Rackspace. They were impressed by his cutting-edge approach towards automation, still uncommon at the time. They invited Eric to their New York conference to share the Showpitch team's forward-thinking methods. The session was very well received and just a month later, they flew him to London to share his message again. More sessions followed soon after.

The back-to-back speaking invitations once again revealed Eric's gift for inspiring others. Public speaking had first sparked his passion as a youth pastor long ago. Now blending technical insights and life wisdom, he had found the sweet spot where his interests converged. On stage, Eric spoke from experience, weaving together code, humanity and humor. His openness resonated across roles and backgrounds. By inviting people into his world, he forged connections at the human core. Should we call him the Pastor of Technology?

Eric was still working for Showpitch and attended Rackspace's conferences as a speaker but, as the startup was not doing too well,

> Now blending technical insights and life wisdom, he had found the sweet spot where his interests converged.

towards the end of his tenure he had to work without pay.

"*In my last two months at the startup, I was actually working without getting paid. I have always been loyal to my work and the company that I have worked for, so despite the fact that I did not get any salary, I continued my work for them. Eventually, my wife confronted me and we discussed our situation. Soon after, I left the job.*"

Eric reached out to Rackspace about job opportunities as Showpitch was struggling to stay afloat. This was a mutual covenant. In 2016, he joined Rackspace as a Solutions Architect and AWS Evangelist. As an AWS Evangelist, he had to be on top of all the latest developments happening on the AWS platform. So, he went ahead and achieved all three AWS Associate level certifications - Solutions Architect, Developer and Sysops Administrator - —in a single week that November. Eric had already been working on AWS for a while, so he was able to briskly scale his learning curve. Cloud technologies were his new doctrine.

Eric also had an early passion for serverless. He heard about AWS Lambda that was announced at re:Invent 2014. Eric instantly recognized serverless computing as the next big thing. He was hooked.

At the time, tools like AWS Serverless Application Model (SAM) and other serverless frameworks did not exist. Undeterred, Eric started scripting and deploying functions all by himself to puzzle out the new offering. When AWS SAM was released, he dove in headfirst, becoming the serverless patriarch at work.

> *I was the serverless guy at Rackspace. I was reading about it all the time, keeping up with any new information. I was even writing about serverless and letting customers know about how this new alternative could work for them the best.*

When serverless bloomed mainstream, Eric was prepared to reap the harvest and lead the way. His early investments in serverless technology ensured expertise few could rival and this soon brought him a golden opportunity.

His co-worker, was contacted by AWS for a Serverless Developer Advocate role. When he went through the Job Description and the required skill set, he realized that Eric had a blend of technical processes and communication strengths that perfectly suited the Developer Advocacy profile. He recommended Eric as an ideal fit for the role.

Eric didn't chase the opportunity, but his dedication to serverless ensured he was discovered. By tending to that specialization with care and sharing it freely, doors opened before him. When Eric read the Job Description, it felt like it was a role written specifically for him. He prepared for the interview like reading a gospel.

> *During the interview process, the main focus was on Amazon's Leadership Principles. Surprisingly, I wasn't asked many technical*

💡 His early investments in serverless technology ensured expertise few could rival and this soon brought him a golden opportunity.

questions. Later I learned this was because they had already researched me thoroughly. They read my articles and blogs and knew my work as a Solutions Architect at Rackspace. They felt I was a strong fit and offered me the Developer Advocate role. My role was to learn about serverless technologies and then share that knowledge with others on various platforms."

This job was a perfect fit for Eric, allowing him to feed his hunger for learning while also continuing his passion for sharing knowledge. The Developer advocate role enabled him to plant seeds of knowledge in others, while cultivating his abilities every day. Eric found his work reminiscent of his days as a youth pastor sharing lessons of faith. Where Eric once guided young minds to find purpose and growth, he now inspired developers to create and innovate.

Though the content had changed from spiritual to technical, the same commitment to educating and uplifting people remained. Eric felt profound fulfilment in helping audiences grasp new concepts and possibilities, much like when he illuminated biblical teachings for youth groups. His ease in front of crowds and gift for explanation traced back to those early days cultivating wisdom and perspective from the pulpit.

Though his tools were now code snippets instead of scripture, Eric brought the same energy and empathy to illuminating complex topics and empowering audiences to dream bigger. His audiences ranged from small meetups to major conferences with thousands of attendees. No matter the crowd size, Eric relished every chance to educate fellow developers on building next-generation apps with serverless.

On the personal front, Eric now resided permanently in Northern Colorado raising his 5 children. His sons are grown up now and he along with his wife home schools their daughters.

"My three boys are just like me in the hands. My oldest daughter has five fingers and my youngest daughter has one finger like us. Interestingly, I'd say my oldest girl feels left out sometimes because she's the odd one out, you know? As the only one with five fingers in our family, she doesn't have that visible shared trait."

"Home schooling our daughters has been an adventure, though not always easy. But we're excited to take the next step in our journey soon. Next year, we plan to put our house up for rent, load the girls into an RV, and live on the roads for a year or year and a half traveling all around the United States. This has been my wife's dream for a long time. She wants to teach the girls history up close by visiting historical sites across the country. We'll have plenty of good stories to tell when it's over!"

This merging of passions suits Eric, who cares deeply about blending humanity and technology. In one of his talk - *Rediscovering*

Humanity in Tech[1] - he takes a light-hearted approach to how humans communicate. By the end of the session, audiences have laughed, maybe even cried, but hopefully grasped the grace we can extend and mercy we can receive as fellow people in the tech world.

"*There is a scripture in Micah 6:8 -* **Do justice, love mercy and walk humbly with God** *- that my grandfather lived by, my dad lived by and I too try to live by. And it simply translates to - be kind in this world.*"

Eric gently reminds us that behind all the code and machines, real human connections matter the most, *family* ties matter the most. Though known for his technical expertise, his message speaks right to the heart. He lives and spreads his belief that technology should uplift our shared humanity, not override it.

Through all of life's twists and turns, Eric remains true to his core values of faith, family, and uses his skills to help others. Though his path took unexpected diversions, he emerged with a richer perspective and a firm sense of his purpose. Now blending his love of technology and teaching, Eric has found the perfect convergence of his passions. His work continues to evolve, but is rooted in the same desire to uplift and empower that first called him to ministry - faith and reason.

As he looks ahead to new adventures on the road ahead, Eric is grateful for the journey so far. His story is a testament to the good that can grow from struggle, and the lives that are touched when we lead with humanity. Though his tools and titles changed over the

---

[1]https://youtu.be/hv4xkrgYknw

years, Eric stayed true to his calling. Through word and deed, he lights the way for others to thrive.

ADVICE

Advice when following a Cloud career path

- **Don't give up easily** - Learning a new thing will always be challenging. If you have a goal in mind, keep trying different paths and continue hammering till you achieve it.

- **Ask questions** - Asking the right questions is a great way of learning. If you don't know – ask. People may shake their heads and roll their eyes, but in the end you will come out with more knowledge.

- **You have just 24 hours in a day** - Invest your time wisely. Don't get dragged in every direction. Learn to say no to things, which does not add up to your long-term goal.

ACTION

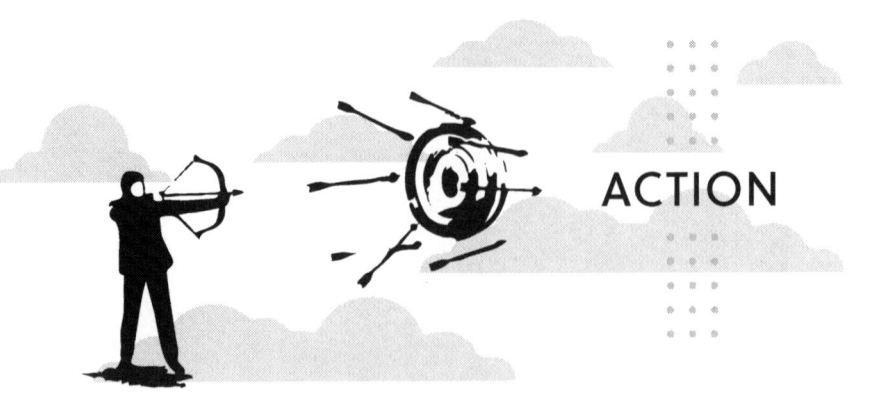

Actions to take that will drive meaningful progress

- **Do, share, teach** - The Do part will get you skills, the Share part will let people know about you, the Teach part will deepen your understanding of the subject and will help others too.

- **Like the next shiny thing** - Always be on a learning journey and look for what is coming next, but don't move to the next thing without finishing the current one.

- **Get Advice** - Talk to people who are in the role you want to get in. Understand the work involved in reaching that position. Get to know the whole job not just the parts you see on the stage.

ALERT

Alerts to avoid common pitfalls that can hinder success

- **Don't just memorize** - Prioritize understanding of the concepts which will ensure you retain that knowledge for long. Remember human brain is not designed to memorize, it is designed for creation.

- **"I know everything syndrome"** - Whatever height you have scaled in your journey there is always room to grow. Don't consider that you know everything. When you think so your growth stops.

- **Putting money over joy** - Make sure you choose your career because you love what you're doing. Otherwise, if it was all for money, soon you will tire you and your journey will be difficult. Figure out what you love to do and then get paid to do it.

The Undefeated

Paved Cloud path against all odds

They regain the trail after detours and persist when the path gets tough. Though setbacks may force them to take a break or change course, these resilient explorers get back on their feet to find new paths to Cloud success.

The Undefeated

The Undefeated

Jamila Jamilova
Solutions Architect,
AWS

04 Chasing Dreams Beyond the Barrier,
Charting Own Course to Cloud Career

Sandip Das
Cloud Architect,
AWS Container Hero

05 Transforming Liabilities into Assets,
Cloud Freelancer Becoming an AWS Hero

Parna Mehta
AWS Authorized Instructor
Technical Trainer, AWS

06 A Break in Career,
A Leap into the Cloud

Pathfinders | **Undefeated** | Progressives | Liberators | Accelerators | Pinnacles

Chasing Dreams Beyond the Barrier, Charting Own Course to Cloud Career

04

Jamila Jamilova

Solutions Architect,
AWS

No dream is too boundless, and no dreamer too insignificant. But dreams don't become reality only through magic. They need to be nurtured through patience, determination, hard work and belief for the magic to happen.

What was Jamila's dream?
How did her dream became a reality?

Sometimes it is hard to imagine what challenges a six-year-old girl is perhaps facing? This is the age when most kids are adored by their parents, pampered (read spoiled), and kept afloat without the knowledge of any complications that are prevailing in the world. Wish this was true for Jamila too. When she started making sense of her existence at the age of six, she realized her parents were divorced, her younger brother was living with her mom, and her father was settling in Russia after his new marriage. She knew from that very moment that her story is going to be atypical.

Throughout an up-and-down upbringing, complete with a debilitating battle with confusion and uncertainty, there was a single consistent thread in her life – Her Grandmother. Jamila's grandmother raised her with love and encouragement in Sumqayit, a small city in

Azerbaijan. She had worked as a professional chef, but left her full-time career to take care of Jamila. She never let young Jamila be lost in the vacuum caused by the divorce of her parents.

While embodying religious and traditional value, she always believed women deserved chances equal to men. Women should be well educated and self-reliant. It was not easy given the cultural norms and traditional expectations from women. But Jamila's grandma was a lady of determination. With love and wisdom, she nurtured Jamila's growth and encouraged her to dream big, despite obstacles.

"*My grandma could not get a higher education as she got married at the age of 16. Despite that, her views about the upliftment of women were way ahead of its time. We were like a team - it was us against the world and sometimes also against my father. She was superior in hierarchy to my father and if he ever judged my choices or my grandma's unconditional love for me, she would interfere and take my side. She had the veto power and never hesitated to exercise it.*"

Despite prevailing social and cultural norms, she forbade Jamila from doing household chores. This allowed Jamila to focus all her attention and energy towards studies. Jamila never let her down; in school she always stood tall and was always the top performer.

At an early age, Jamila was uncertain about what to aim for, as women had limited career options in her country. Still, her

> With love and wisdom, she nurtured Jamila's growth and encouraged her to dream big, despite obstacles.

grandmother always had her back. Jamila's grandma was her anchor against storms of doubt. Her supportive guidance helped Jamila gain the strength to chart her course. Together, the duo of granddaughter and grandmother persevered. Though the path was hard, they walked it with faith.

"*My grandma believed in me all the time, even if others did not. As she was religious, she always asked me to work hard, have faith and pray. She encouraged me to take action towards my dreams, desires, and plans.*"

Growing up in Azerbaijan, Jamila initially aspired to become a pediatrician. This dream was inspired by a foreign-trained doctor, who successfully treated her chronic cough. He diagnosed her chronic cough, revealing a hidden allergy that other doctors missed to identify. Jamila was so impressed that she wanted to study medicine abroad at a top university, just like him, and be a specialist in the medical field.

Jamila was a teenager in a small city where the biggest achievement for someone was getting into the university in the capital, Baku and building a life there. That was considered the pinnacle of success, especially for a woman. But Jamila never wanted that to be her end goal. She always dreamed of living in London instead. Somehow the red buses, the old architectures and the telephone booths, charmed her. Wasn't it too big a dream for a small-town girl?

"*I wanted to become a doctor in Germany or Turkey and then live in London eventually. But my father did not agree to send me to a foreign country to study alone. He suggested that I continue my* studies at Azerbaijan or at a low-ranked university in Russia where my father lived with his new family."

"I wasn't happy with this decision. So, after the disagreement with my father, I lost my focus on studies. There was a shift in my mindset. I thought if I cannot get what I want then what's the point of even making the effort."

In the crucial months before the final exams, this disappointment distracted Jamila. She was a bright student all these years but in the end terms her focus wavered, and her scores slipped. She was not able to get admission in any medical colleges in Baku.

After her dreams of going to a medical school shattered miserably, Jamila found herself in a place of failure and uncertainty. However, she came across an opportunity to study ecology at Azerbaijan State University of Economics in Baku.

"Environmental Ecology was actually being introduced into the University of Economics for the first time that year when I applied for it. It was a government funded initiative to study about environmental issues. I received monthly stipends. As my grades improved the amount of the stipend increased gradually."

While paving her own way through the ecology program, Jamila networked across the university in her first year. Though she enjoyed her studies, a question lingered - what jobs could this degree lead to?

Though medicine had been her childhood dream, this redirection revealed new possibilities. Out of the uncertainty came a chance to rediscover her academic calling. Where one door closed, another opened for Jamila to flourish in studies and redefine her goals.

A math teacher, impressed by Jamila's drive and grades, told her about the International Economy course. There, professors with global experience taught courses that reignited Jamila's desire for world-class education. Jamila now yearned to study International Economy and applied to the program. After some assessments, she got admission into International Economy classes in her second year of university. Dreamt of studying in a medical college, ended up in a course in Environmental Ecology for the first year in college, and now thinking about International Economy? What exactly was she doing?

"*So far my classes were taught in Russian, but these International Economy classes were in advanced English - far exceeding my below average English skills. The textbooks reflected foreign education standards, dense with statistics and econometrics that overwhelmed me. I really needed help to pass and ended up looking for it!*"

The math teacher who had helped get Jamila into the program came into the rescue again! She connected Jamila with her son, who was studying economics at LSE (London school of economics). With her teacher's insistence, Jamila contacted him through Facebook and asked him for some help. As Jamila found answers to her academic questions, their conversations broadened. Soon they spoke of future plans, envisioning a shared path.

"*My math teacher, who is also my mother-in-law now, linked me and my husband. Her son was doing his Masters at the time and had future plans for doing his PhD from abroad. Our goals in life and career were similar. We felt an instant spark and were a perfect match for each other."*

Jamila and her teacher's son got engaged. As he applied to PhD programs worldwide, Jamila secretly hoped he would get into a program in London. Her long-held dream of living in London now seemed possible. By the time his fiancé's acceptance letters from university arrived, they were married. Soon after, he was admitted in London Business School. Jamila's prayers materialized - her destination dream would now come true.

Though not yet done with her bachelor's degree, Jamila eagerly headed to London to begin her new life. She traveled between Azerbaijan and the UK to finish her studies while embarking on her and her husband's next chapter.

As the old saying goes - *When you want something, the whole universe conspires in order for you to achieve it.* For Jamila, the universe aligned to bring her to London by drawing the right people and chances into her orbit. Her dream called out, and the world answered back. The city that captured her imagination as a child became her destiny through the unfoldment of life's magic.

She was soon marvelling at the bustling streets of London. Despite all the charm and opportunities, a big city offers, settling in can be difficult initially. How was Jamila going to face it? Would she be affected by it? Has she been dreaming of the right thing?

In their early years in London, Jamila and her husband lived in student accommodation. Jamila looked for work. Her English wasn't fluent yet, but she had an edge – she could speak Russian. As a resident rather than a visitor, Jamila's relationship with London transformed. Casual tourism gave way to digging deeper roots. She explored pragmatic needs – income, community, purpose.

"I applied for jobs at high end jewelery stores like Tiffany's that hire customer service agents who could speak many languages. But in interviews, my broken English failed me. I decided to take English classes to improve. But it was expensive and did not align with our student budget."

When Jamila's daughter was almost one year old, they were still living in the university campus. Here, Jamila got an opportunity to volunteer with the student community of the University of London. This short experience helped improve her spoken English. Interacting with students boosted her confidence. It was a small but valuable opportunity to practice and improve her English.

She got a part time job as a salesperson at the healthcare product store. Initially she was sceptical about the job. Did she complete a degree in International Economy for a store salesperson job?

Jamila started to learn on the job about sales and started promoting a specific product line in the store. Though the product was of great quality, it was not drawing as much sales as expected. She started looking into avenues to grow the customer base. She compared the historical sales data of similar products and realized that there was demand, but somehow this product was not channelising into that stream. What could be the problem then?

She soon realized that this could be because of the placement of the product. As it was not properly placed in Point of purchase (POP). A point of purchase is a marketing term used to describe the area of high visibility in the store, where most customers make purchase decisions. It is the area where most customers will encounter the products, so placing it there can increase the chances of people buying it.

"*I was confident that I could improve sales with just the right placement of the products but my suggestions were overlooked. I did not budge and was willing to prove my point with data. But there were so many data points, and I wanted to consider all of it before coming to a conclusion after my initial analysis. I am not a human calculator, so I had to crunch these numbers using a computer. But even I get hold of a computer how am I going to analyse the data?*"

She did not have any means to engage a team of data scientists sitting in the corporate HQ. Even if she approached them, the chances of them looking at it seemed very slim. She is just a store salesperson, started few months back and has little or no experience of the whole dynamics of sales cycle. She should bury down that thought and just focus on her work. Right?

"*I was not going to back down. Without any possibility of external help, it was time to roll up the sleeves and get things done. I did my initial research and I would need some data analytics tools and bit or programming knowledge. I started learning Microsoft Excel, SQL and Python for data analysis on my own initially. I watched videos on YouTube from wise owl tutorials[1] and learned from their data*

---

[1] https://www.youtube.com/@WiseOwlTutorials/videos

analysis of Titanic Shipwreck. I also continued learning by building projects from sites like Kaggle[1] to enhance my understanding."

Jamila did extra work with no expectation of more pay or promotion. She started to boost sales, driven by her initiative to improve the business. Data has become her new tool. She became more engaged with analyzing data than her sales role. She had drifted into IT unintentionally, yet the winds kept propelling her onward. An Area Manager was impressed with her work which she accomplished without any support. When an opening surfaced in the data analytics team at HQ, she secured an interview for her. The stars were aligning.

"The founders of the company were impressed with my efforts to better the sales process of the company. I was given a free hand to choose the department of my choice and use my analytical thinking and data driven approach to upgrade the process of that department. I was able to live up to their expectations" Soon after, she started to search for a role in the technology field and appeared in an interview for a customer analyst role at a startup. During her interview she was told that she was overqualified - her SQL and data skills exceeded the job description. They advised her to aim higher. She was just starting in IT by chance, when did she become overqualified?"

She did not deter, and kept applying for other jobs. She got hired as a Support Engineer in a fintech company. As a new Support Engineer, Jamila often explained solutions to customers. But when she faced backend platform issues, she forwarded it to the Infrastructure Engineer for a resolution. As she learned that their backend systems

---
[1] https://www.kaggle.com/

were hosted on AWS Cloud, she got eager to grasp Cloud computing fundamentals despite her unfamiliarity. She was driven by curiosity to troubleshoot the technical problems herself.

"When the Engineer informed me that our solutions use AWS, I wanted to learn about it. We talked about the AWS workforce of talented people who have built those services. I was immediately intrigued and aspired to work at AWS one day. I started diving deep to learn about AWS and asked him to guide me. Seeing my curiosity and eagerness to learn he started teaching me in weekly sessions."

"Another co-worker, introduced me to AWS certifications. He advised me to achieve AWS Certified Solutions Architect Associate certification to build skills. While preparing, I came across A Cloud Guru course and it helped me immensely to learn AWS."

While things were settling for Jamila, COVID-19 pandemic started crimpling the global market. After over a year at the fintech, Jamila got laid off as the company downsized. With her redundancy payout, she bought a laptop and continued learning AWS. She was now dreaming of working at AWS someday. Another dream.

Jamila applied for multiple jobs at AWS through LinkedIn. She created a document called "AWS Interview" to add notes, hoping to use it when her resume would get shortlisted. She was applying extensively to all kinds of roles at AWS and got worried that she might come across as a spammer. But after learning about the Solutions Architect role, she got laser focused on it. Its non-technical aspects of analysis, creativity, critical thinking, customer communication fit her strengths.

In her period of unemployment and financial strain, she had focused solely on AWS. Her loved ones urged her to apply to other companies too as getting into AWS was not an easy feat. But Jamila remained resolute in her AWS dream despite their concerns. She would not lose sight of her goal.

"I started growing my network on LinkedIn and connected with AWS employees. Within a community of shared interest, vital relationships can develop and guide your journey. I requested mentorship from experienced AWS employees who assured me to not pressurize myself over things which I am yet to learn. I was told that it is possible to have a gap in our understanding of certain technical concepts but it gets cleared over time with experience."

Jamila's networking on LinkedIn led an AWS Hiring manager inviting her to a technical interview for a solutions architect role. She thought - Is this actually happening?

Previously unaware of the hiring process, Jamila followed an ex-Amazon director posting newsletters about Amazon interview processes and the Amazon leadership principles. This offered some insight before her first round with the Hiring Manager.

"*I was nervous for my first interview round. When I was sharing my experience and my learning from my previous job role, I had jumbled up between situations. But my interviewer informed me that I should follow a structured STAR format - describing the Situation, Task, Action, and Result in my explanations. And I kept this advice in mind for all my further interview rounds.*"

After clearing initial screening rounds, it was time for Jamila to prepare for the AWS loop interview. The loop interview consists of 5 successive interviews. It enables layered assessment from different viewpoints and is mainly focussed on Amazon Leadership Principles.[1]

"*When I appeared for my loop interview, I was super focused on doing well. I didn't let doubts in. I used learning from previous interviews and prepared well. I saw that really deep answers matter more than you'd think. Sometimes they wanted every tiny detail of my previous work experience explained with the nitty gritties. They also checked for leadership skills in all my answers.*"

Jamila waited eagerly for the outcome, and she was not disappointed. She succeeded against the odds. She had no IT background, minimal AWS knowledge, almost no hands-on experience and zero AWS certifications yet she aced the interview for the role of Solutions Architect. But without technical expertise or years of experience,

---

[1] https://www.amazon.jobs/en/principles

how did Jamila clear the rigorous AWS interview process?

"I demonstrated strong culture fit with Amazon. They are known for hiring people who align with their leadership principles. My recruiter said the most crucial ones for AWS Solutions Architects are Learn and Be Curious, Earn Trust and Dive Deep. In the stories I shared about my experiences, I highlighted how those principles shaped my approach."

During interviews, Jamila could showcase the drive to add value in innovative ways. For instance, as a salesperson Jamila independently learned data analysis to boost company sales. This demonstrated *Learn and Be Curious* as she picked up skills beyond her core job and *Earn Trust* by transparently elevating performance with evidence. Later as a Support Engineer unfamiliar with AWS, Jamila proactively sought Cloud computing knowledge, illustrating *Learn and Be Curious* again. Here she also showcased *Dive Deep* by troubleshooting issues herself.

Her self-motivation and ingenuity earned trust. Jamila's range of self-taught abilities proved that she would continue to strive for excellence. Jamila's past determination was a testament to the future impact she could make. Finally, Jamila had attained a job in her dream city, with her dream company – childhood dreams do come true.

"My early days at AWS was a steep learning curve. Within two weeks, I passed the AWS Certified Solutions Architect Associate

> During interviews, Jamila could showcase the drive to add value in innovative ways.

certification. I grasped new terms and "Amazonian" traits along the way. Within first year I went on to gain my AWS Certified Solutions Architect Professional certification. Next, I achieved AWS Certified Security Speciality certification, followed by the challenging Database Specialty - my hardest exam yet. The choice to achieve these specific certifications was driven by the customer engagements I was handling."

At first overwhelmed and enamoured with every aspect of her role, Jamila overloaded her plate, eager for each project. But gradually, she learned to prioritize quality over quantity of output. Deeply appreciating the value of mentorship, Jamila benefited from guidance early on at AWS. She was fortunate to receive this support especially from senior women colleagues. Their wisdom blessed her budding career.

"I have always been inspired by women in leading positions in a company. And I am well aware that a lot of women like me derive inspiration from each other. I purposefully try and mentor women and people from underrepresented groups and disadvantaged background. I love giving back to the community and help people who are in the position I was when I started. And that's the reason I decided to co-found BeSA (Become a Solutions Architect) Program[1] with my peers, a free mentoring initiative, which helps people to excel in their Cloud career journeys."

> *I purposefully try and mentor women and people from underrepresented groups and disadvantaged background.*

---

[1] https://become-a-solutions-architect.github.io

Jamila has been working with AWS for two and a half years now and has worked in three different teams as a Solutions Architect. She currently helps start-ups build and scale on the AWS, a role she loves.

Jamila has travelled far, from a small-town girl dreaming of big cities to settling in bustling London. She has known failure but rebuilt hope each time like a phoenix rising. Jamila does not lose hope, she architects it. To Jamila, a dream is a wish, a possibility, and a chance to change one's life.

Jamila stands as inspiration, transformed by daring dreams. She shows that improbable dreams can manifest through passion and grit. She encourages others to follow their dreams while also growing personally and professionally.

ADVICE

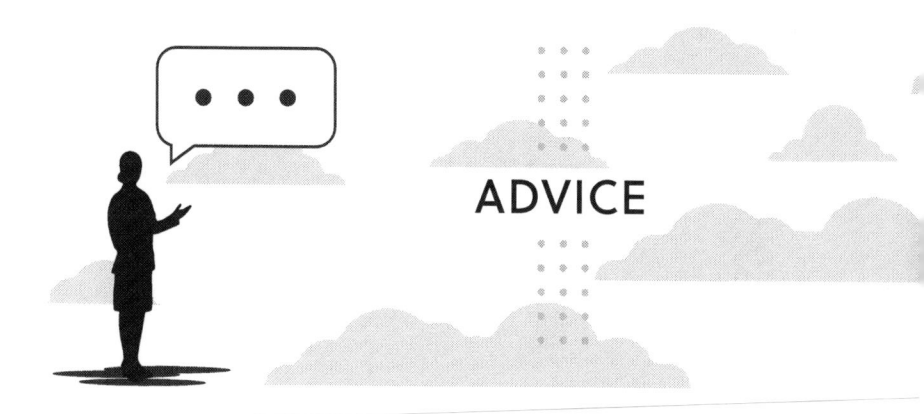

Advice when following a Cloud career path

- **Know exactly what you want** - Understand why a particular industry or role appeals to you. Defining your dreams with clarity and conviction will help guide your career.

- **Don't give up on your passions** - Hold on to your passions and keep working towards it even if you don't see any opportunities at the moment. Success occurs when opportunities meet preparation.

- **Explore your options** - If you are completely clueless about which industry is your calling. Keep exploring your options and build your interests along the way.

ACTION

Actions to take that will drive meaningful progress

- **Attend free in-person or virtual Cloud events** - It will help you to gauge your interest in specific technologies. You will have plenty of opportunities to do hands-on workshops led by experts.

- **Connect with like-minded people** - Purposefully connect with people whose interests are aligned with yours. Talk to them with respect. Share your passions. Listen to their stories.

- **Do hands-on activity** - Build projects to sharpen your skillset. You can find free online projects to get started. Strengthen your knowledge through hands-on activities.

ALERT

Alerts to avoid common pitfalls that can hinder success

- **Starting without foundational knowledge** - The Cloud offers immense possibilities, but start small. Focus first on mastering the fundamentals before diving deeper.

- **Don't bite off more than you can chew** - Don't overcommit to projects beyond your current skills and bandwidth. Know your limits and accordingly pace yourself.

- **Randomly seeking help** - Thoughtful preparation increases the odds of a favorable response. Learn about the person, see how they can assist, and approach respectfully with a specific ask.

Transforming Liabilities into Assets, Cloud Freelancer Becoming an AWS Hero

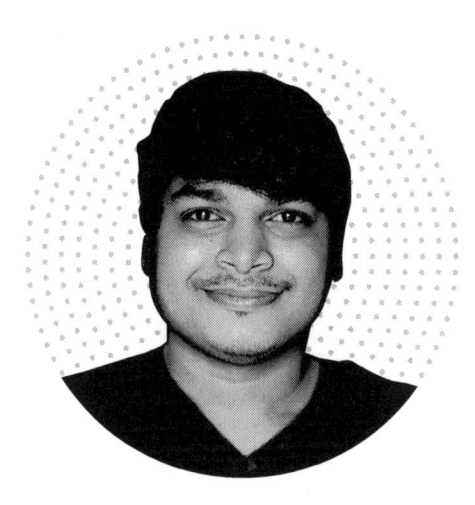

05

Sandip Das
Cloud Architect,
AWS Container Hero

Whether it is a multibillion-dollar business or a lone freelancer, they all try to accumulate assets and reduce liabilities in their financial balance-sheet. We all individually maintain an invisible balance sheet for our life too.

How does the balance sheet of an AWS Cloud Hero looks like? Can he turn liabilities into assets?

E ach specific life comes with its own personalized portion of pain. The ones deprived of privileges often strive the most to succeed in life. They do not crumble under the hardship handed to them but rather grow beyond it through perseverance and hard work. Sandip was born and raised in the impoverished neighbourhoods of Howrah City in West Bengal, India. He was the younger of two sons. His father worked as a metal shaper and his mother sold handcrafted toys to pull together extra earnings to manage the household. Growing up, Sandip bitterly witnessed poverty up close. His early childhood memories were filled with the struggles he and his family faced just to survive.

"*Our household income was below poverty line for a long time. We faced constant financial crises as we made a living for ourselves.*

I have a memory written down on a piece of paper from my early childhood. It was when the roof of our house had blown away because of a thunderstorm and our family was left soaking wet in the rain. My naivety made me question my mother on why our roof was not strong like our neighbors' houses. To which my mother had replied that we could not afford it. That incident stuck with me as a constant reminder of the hardship we endured."

This initial struggle fuelled Sandip's motivation to build a better life and future for those he loved. He believed that there is one person in every household who can change the financial fate of his or her family. He challenged himself in becoming that person. Was he able to live up to that challenge?

"*When I used to brew these desires one thing which my parents always taught me was to walk on the right path of morality. It was easier to get caught up in bad habits in the places where I come from but I have always stood by principles my parents instilled in me.*"

Sandip grew up in the shadow of a real-life hero - his older brother. When their family hit financial rock bottom, his older brother sacrificed his education to nourish Sandip's potential. He dropped out of school to work, in order to support Sandip's studies. Sandip remained rooted in the school and studied diligently.

Though Sandip did not have the luxury to go to a fancy school or to go to a private tutor for his studies, he was trying his best to manage studies. In this struggle, his uncle's friend Sovan Samadder, who was a chartered accountant by profession, saw yearning and potential in Sandip. He helped him and initially started tutoring, and later supported financially for his education. He funded his entire education all the way from early school through college graduation. This left an everlasting impression on Sandip, and that is how his uncle's friend became his role model for the life.

"Sovan uncle was a Chartered Accountant by profession. So, when I had to pick between Science, Arts, and Commerce for higher studies, I picked Commerce as it meant free tuition from him. I wanted to study Science but I didn't have the money or resources to pursue Science at the time. I knew Commerce would help me gain skills for becoming an accountant, just like my role model. I decided to be practical and choose the subject area that made the most sense in my situation."

He started to understand basic principles from his role model cum tutor cum supporter. His *balance sheet* was shaping up.

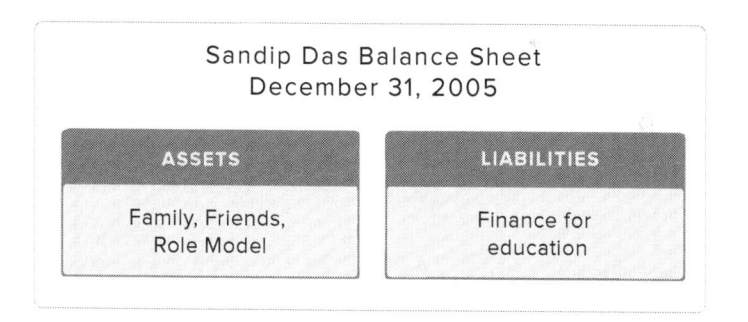

Sandip Das Balance Sheet
December 31, 2005

ASSETS	LIABILITIES
Family, Friends, Role Model	Finance for education

While in higher secondary school, Sandip's teachers advised him to learn computer skills at the nearby community Computer center, which offered classes for free. Sandip initially enrolled in it out of curiosity. He learned about computer hardware and networking, programming, UI and UX designing. Sandip got his first taste of computer technology at this institute. Little did he know that this will be a turning point in his life. When and how is he going to achieve a *break-even* first, and start showing *profitability*?

"*After doing well in school, it was time for me to start working towards a bachelor's degree. Since I had studied Commerce, I decided to enrol in a Bachelor of Commerce program. But just getting to college every day was a huge challenge. My university was across the Hooghly River in Kolkata, while I lived in Howrah. To get there, I had to take a ferry across the dividing waters between the cities, and then catch a bus to campus. Overall, it was 4 hours commute every day.*"

On top of the commute time, his parents could scarcely spare the everyday travel cost. Sandip knew this and was reluctant to burden them when finances were already stretched thin at home. How he is going to maintain the already dwindling *cash-flow*?

"*I got a job at a call center working in night shift. This helped me earn money to cover my travel costs for college. As this call center supported foreign clients, talking with them also helped me improve my English language skills. I enjoyed the challenge of having conversations with people spanning continents and cultures.*"

Sandip worked at the call center through college, squirreling away small *capital investments* while providing for his family. The job allowed him to plant seeds for his own future. When choosing Commerce as a choice for studies years before, Sandip had sacrificed his personal interests due to limited means. Now, with resources slowly growing, he cultivated a long-held passion - technology. Sandip enrolled in a three-year MCA (Master of Computer Applications) program through IGNOU (Indira Gandhi National

Open University). This allowed him to branch out from commerce into computer science, his true calling. He was diversifying his time in hope of a better *returns-on-the-investment (ROI)*.

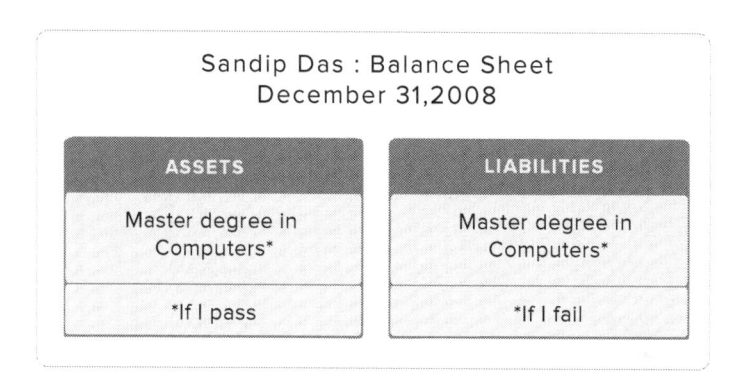

Sandip Das : Balance Sheet
December 31, 2008

ASSETS	LIABILITIES
Master degree in Computers*	Master degree in Computers*
*If I pass	*If I fail

Learning different computer skills is one thing and passing a Masters degree is another. Will he be able to pass a Master's degree?

"*Switching from Commerce to IT proved challenging for me. In first year of the MCA program, I failed all eight subjects, underestimating the depth of technology. I reached a potential mental insolvency. I was trying to study while working in the night shift at the call center. This failure shouldn't have surprised me, but it sure as hell disappointed me.*"

In year two, Sandip righted his course. He had to get rid of the technical *debt*. He enrolled in computer coaching classes and leaned on friends with computer science backgrounds. He was *budgeting* his call center salary carefully. With proper guidance and support, Sandip cleared his backlogs and passed all subjects that year - even the eight retakes. By the third year, Sandip felt equipped to self-study. He had to stop coaching classes, and use his time for freelance work of web development in order to sustain financially. Sandip felt that he had cultivated the knowledge needed to thrive independently in IT. A night shift call center job, a distance education Master's degree and now a venture in freelancing, isn't he taking too much *risk*?

"*I started freelancing in web development, but lacked skills for advanced projects. To gain professional experience, I left my call center job and joined an IT company as a junior developer. During my 7 months there, I got experience with JavaScript and improved my understanding of programming fundamentals. I relied heavily on senior colleagues to learn and progress from a beginner to a capable Web Developer. I was fortunate to find people who were willing to help me.*"

Eager to continue challenging himself, Sandip switched jobs once more in pursuit of more demanding work and better *compensation*. He was determined to keep accumulating *asset* of knowledge in the *balance sheet* of his career. Each role allowed Sandip to deepen his technical skills and soak up new knowledge. Will he ever get *dividend* on the *investment* he is making?

"*Juggling a full-time job while finishing my MCA proved difficult. In my first attempt at the final exams, I was unable to pass all subjects. But I took some months to really focus on studying, then tried the exams again. With a lot of determination, I was able to complete my master's degree on the second attempt.*"

Sandip's third and final corporate IT job led him to crossroads. As a Senior Web Developer, he honed technical and client communication skills, but for this job, he had to commute almost 8-hours every day.

This exhausted him, wilting his health. It was a tough time for him to make a decision. He had been freelancing on the side, and now felt ready to sustain independently.

"The daily commute was taking a toll on my health. I had enough savings to survive without a regular monthly income till my freelancing work could progress to earn me a living. So, I took a stern decision and quit my job . I started leveraging platforms like Upwork and Freelancer to find projects. My first opportunity came from Steve, an elderly man looking to build an interactive video platform."

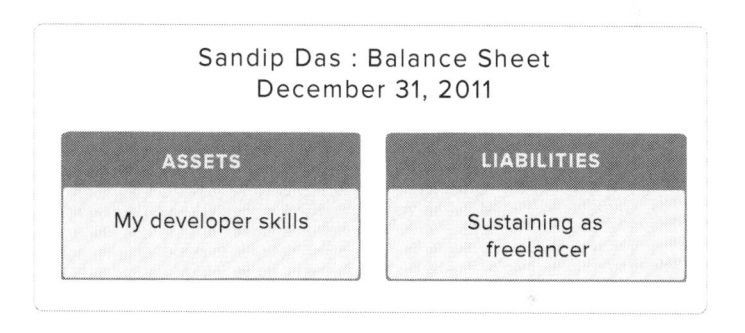

Sandip Das : Balance Sheet
December 31, 2011

ASSETS	LIABILITIES
My developer skills	Sustaining as freelancer

Like a sapling maturing into a mighty oak, Sandip felt capable to stand tall alone. He had absorbed all he could from these jobs and was ready to start his own venture and be his own boss. With extensive PHP, JavaScript, and automation experience, Sandip readily took on the ambitious project. Steve was so impressed, he referred much more work Sandip's way - proof that happy clients are the best source of new opportunities. Sandip had made the right investment in fostering a strong relationship with his customer. This customer was one of the major customer for Sandip, but he still worked for others too. He was his own boss and his own time manager.

"*As a freelancer you can't just depend on one source of income from one client. You have to diversify and be prepared for change of events to keep your work and business functioning. Your client or customer may bring you more work in the future when they recommend your good work to others. I vividly remember that in a particular month I have worked almost 18 to 20 hours each day. In that month I earned enough money to pay sufficient deposit for a new house. Finally, I was going to get a house with strong roof.*"

Sandip became the person, who changed the financial fate of his family. This new found financial stability did not alter his ego and he stayed humble to the core. He had not forgotten the sacrifices of his family, and the help he received from his role model, friends and colleagues.

After two years of freelancing, Sandip landed a major project from a new client. They were in early development, allowing Sandip to join as a founding Engineer. Over time, he developed a smart router with parental control per their requirements. However, the product lacked scalability. Sandip advised that an experienced Cloud Engineer could improve scalability of the application. But instead of hiring one, the client empowered Sandip to upskill himself in Cloud computing on his own timeline. They were willing to *invest* on him knowing his skills and attitude.

"*I was asked to learn about Cloud Computing to increase the

> You have to diversify and be prepared for change of events to keep your work and business functioning.

scalability of the application. AWS Cloud was the biggest player in the market of Cloud and I started learning all of its services relevant to solve the issue which my clients were facing. I had the company of another Engineer from the client side and together we learned about AWS services. We were able to stabilize the application by introducing auto scaling and load balancing features."

While learning AWS Cloud computing, Sandip discovered AWS certifications through his involvement in a learning community. His client happily sponsored the training and certifications costs, so Sandip aimed for credentials relevant to his work. He started by visiting the official AWS training pages, mapping out available certifications. Afterwards he turned to platforms like A Cloud Guru and Udemy for the online courses. Sandip left no stone unturned, he read blogs, watched YouTube videos, and scoured technical whitepapers for quality Cloud training content. There were new entries being added in his *balance sheet*.

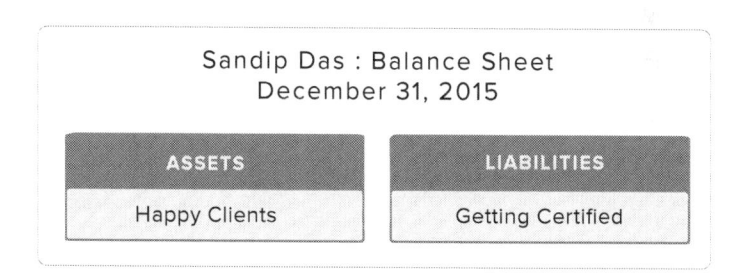

Sandip Das : Balance Sheet	
December 31, 2015	
ASSETS	**LIABILITIES**
Happy Clients	Getting Certified

"*Even with ample resources, I failed my first AWS Certified Cloud Practitioner certification exam. It was easy to cut the losses and write-off the attempt, but I was not going to do that. I focused on my studies, closed the knowledge gaps and passed it in my second attempt. After that I went for the AWS Certified Developer Associate* certification and passed it without any issue. Next was AWS Certified SysOps Administrator Associate - success again!"

"But when I first attempted for AWS Certified Solutions Architect Associate certification, I came up short once more. I took time to gain more hands-on experience at work before trying again. Working on the chat application helped me with certification-worthy knowledge. When I reattempted the AWS Solutions Architect Associate certification exam 6 months later, I was ready and I finally earned that credential as well."

Afterwards, in addition to these AWS Associate certifications, Sandip also attained AWS Certified Solutions Architect Professional and AWS Certified DevOps Engineer Professional certification. Sandip's certification journey had challenges, but he learned from each attempt. When he failed an exam, he used it to identify areas needing more preparation and started to dive deep. Sandip would then work hard to improve missing knowledge before trying again. Bit by bit, he sculpted himself into a Cloud computing expert. What was his learning in this certification journey?

"I don't think it's a good idea to rush through certifications without real on-the-job experience. A Cloud Engineer's certification journey shouldn't be a race just to collect credentials. It's about truly mastering the skills. If you get certified too fast and don't have the

> *It's about truly mastering the skills. If you get certified too fast and don't have the hands-on background, you won't perform well when hired.*

hands-on background, you won't perform well when hired. This can make your certifications look meaningless."

"I believe it's better to take a steady, step-by-step approach. Get practical experience along the way. Prove you have the knowledge the credentials represent. Rushing through exams just for the sake of having them on your resume won't make you qualified. The right way is to combine proper training with real-world Cloud projects. Let your skills truly develop before chasing the next certification."

While preparing for certifications, Sandip joined AWS community groups to stay updated and build connections. He noticed a lack of quality learning resources for newcomers in the Cloud. Seeking to fill this gap, Sandip documented his own AWS journey through YouTube videos and social media posts on LinkedIn. He created content for beginners on AWS core services, and other relevant topics. After covering the basics, Sandip progressed to advanced topics like DevOps and Containers.

He nurtured the community with his knowledge, and helped others grow. He fostered an increasingly abundant investment opportunities for anyone seeking to invest their time in learning AWS skills. Sandip embraced the chance to nourish fellow Cloud enthusiasts just starting their journeys. Sandip's tireless contributions and tenacity to help others resulted into AWS recognizing him as an AWS Hero

> *Rushing through exams just for the sake of having them on your resume won't make you qualified. The right way is to combine proper training with real-world Cloud projects.*

- a title reserved for those who significantly contributes to the AWS community.

"When I joined AWS community group, I yielded many benefits from them. And I wanted to give back to the community in my own way. I wanted the content that I have produced to be available and accessible to everyone free of cost, that is why I never joined hands with any edtech firm to reap profits out of it. Surprisingly, the officials at AWS noticed my efforts and rewarded me with AWS Hero title which I am utterly grateful for."

Sandip traversed a long road from studying accounting, working at call centres, to IT jobs, to running his own freelance business. Early on, he overworked himself juggling multiple client projects. Over time, he found balance in freelancing, creating a stress-free schedule for himself. Looking ahead, he plans to establish a company fully dedicated to Cloud computing, drawing on his seasoned expertise. But for now, he is focused on work-life balance. Sandip makes sure to prioritize time for his family amidst his busy schedule.

While not without struggles, Sandip's life has been defined by diligence and perseverance. He gives back as much knowledge as he has gained, selflessly guiding others in Cloud computing. Sandip transitioned from hardship into success through tireless dedication. His willingness to uplift fellow Cloud enthusiasts has undoubtedly made him a hero. He is compiling his Balance Sheet for 2023.

Sandip Das : Balance Sheet
December 31, 2023

ASSETS	LIABILITIES
Family, Friends, Role Model	~~Help others in learning Cloud*~~
Master degree in Computers	
My developer skills	
Happy Clients	
AWS Certifications	
AWS Hero Award	
Help others in learning Cloud*	

* "I consider this as an asset not a liability."

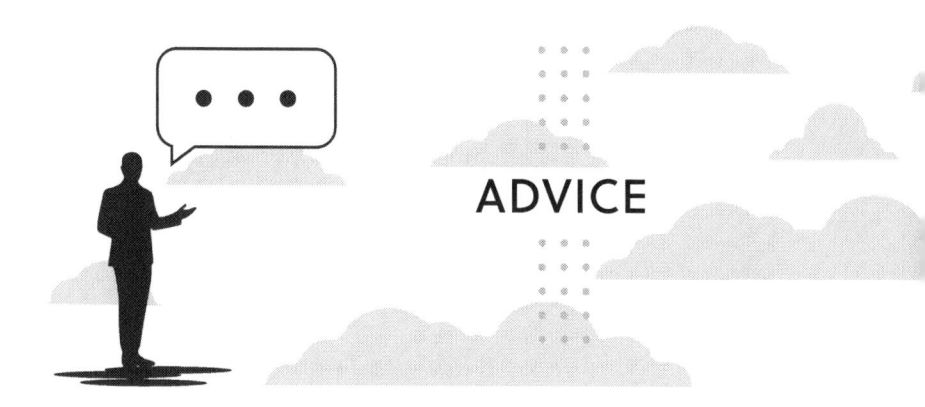

Advice when following a Cloud career path

- **Understand the basics** - Compute, Storage, Database, Networking & Security are the fundamentals of Cloud. If you master this then you can easily conquer the Cloud Services.

- **Add value to your certifications** - Don't jump from one certification to another. Wisely choose the path of your certification journey and do a hands-on practical learning of the contents in each of your certifications.

- **Share what you have learned and achieved in your journey** - When you share your journey with the others, your work and your certifications will get recognised and may reach to the right kind of people who are looking for someone like you to hire.

ACTION

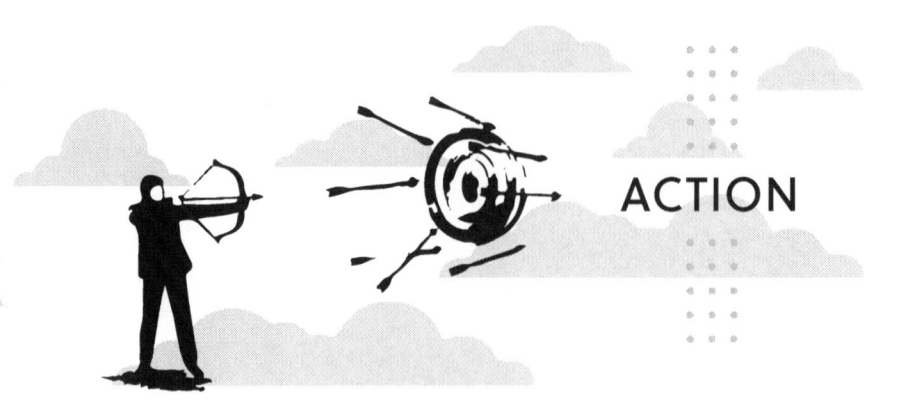

Actions to take that will drive meaningful progress

- **Use the available resources** - Whether it is for learning purposes or interviews make the best use of all the available resources which are out there and fully prepare yourself.

- **Practice your work** - You can only get better at your skills if you regularly practice what you are learning. Make notes of the things you have learned so far or the projects you have worked on and revisit them after some time to practise it again.

- **Grow your network and connections** - You should develop the skill of networking. This skillset is tremendously useful. It can also help you in finding a mentor who can properly guide you in your Cloud journey.

ALERT

Alerts to avoid common pitfalls that can hinder success

- **Procrastination is the enemy of hard work** - You may already be aware of the steps which are needed to be taken to upskill yourself but you delay them and keep important work aside. Don't fall into this trap of stalling, it hinders with your growth.

- **Avoid preaching without practise** - If you only have a theoretical knowledge try to also learn about the practical application of it. In your career your capability will be tested based on your practical knowledge.

- **Don't get disheartened with others successes** - Everybody is in their own journey. We should not get demotivated by the achievements of the others. Your time will come and your work or skills will be recognized but you don't have to live and work for those approvals rather you should only focus on upskilling yourself.

Pathfinders | **Undefeated** | Progressives | Liberators | Accelerators | Pinnacles

A Break in Career,
A Leap into the Cloud

06

Parna Mehta
AWS Authorized Instructor
Technical Trainer, AWS

They say there's always light at the end of the tunnel, but not once your eyes adjust to the darkness. A 12-year career break can be a long tunnel and you would need laser sharp focus and resolute determination to egress from it.

Were the odds stacked sky high against her?

Like every child born in a typical Indian family, Parna had to adhere to the standards and expectations her parents and society had for her. Though these were not willingly forced upon her, children often face pressures to conform to such preset notions about ideal career choices during their upbringing.

Parna spent her childhood in Mumbai, which is considered the economic capital of India, and famous for the widest suburban commuter network in Asia. Probably, anyone living or visiting the city has traversed its lengthy local railway tracks and crowded coaches. These local trains act as the city's lifeline. It was part of Parna's daily life too. As a typical Mumbaikar (people who are native to Mumbai) Parna loved riding the bustling local trains growing up, as this was the fastest means of transport in the city. She commuted to school and college via these along with her sisters. Sometimes, she traveled with just her friends as well. Being the youngest of the three sisters, she was pampered by her parents and benefited from their relaxed rules.

"*My mother made sure that we "Powerpuff girls" had access to everything we needed. She held a Master's degree in Science and very well understood the importance of education for anyone's development. At the same time, my mother also recognized the value of succeeding in extracurricular activities. She was our biggest supporter no matter what we chose to pursue, firmly believing in our comprehensive growth - not just academic achievement.*"

Parna's mother married young and despite studying in a prestigious Indian university, she was unable to fully utilize her education. Nevertheless, she was determined to send her daughters onto express tracks towards top colleges. Parna's father provided the optimal power that kept the family's engine rolling.

"*My father, a self-made man, had always been a provider for the five of us, his parents and younger siblings. He worked hard as a Chartered Accountant and tried his level best to give us a comfortable life in spite of other responsibilities. My father was a doting dad and I don't remember him ever saying no to any of us sisters.*"

Parna was always an excellent student and a top performer in her class. Her favourite subjects used to be Mathematics and Biology.

"*I used to spend hours solving math problems and understanding biology while literally ignoring other subjects. Seeing me excel *academically my parents had ambitious dreams for me."*

When it came to choosing a career, as an 'intelligent' child in urban India, the options narrowed like different train tracks merging into only two tracks - Engineering or Medicine. More than a choice, these two professions were seen as alternatives on the same predetermined journey. Venturing beyond those rigid rails at that time was seen as taboo (and perhaps it still is seen that way).

Loving Mathematics also meant a natural inclination for computers, after all its just zeros and ones, isn't it? To add on, it was (and probably is) considered, possessing a computer science degree was a sure shot for success - a fast train to the destination. This is what set the track for her to pursue only one direction and embark on a focused journey to become an Engineer.

"The other reason I chose to become a Computer Engineer was the opportunity to travel overseas which I heard was a perk in this field. Computer Engineering itself was enjoyable, or maybe I should say college in general was fun. I made a lot of friends and had a good time while still maintaining strong grades."

While India was riding the IT wave, companies had to scramble for talented freshers, who could be trained and take up positions to support off-shore operations. Campus placements allowed these companies access to a fresh pool of talent. Every train system needs commuters, right? Parna got her first job through campus placement in one of the prominent software companies of that time. The Career Express was gaining momentum.

TRAIN NAME - CAREER EXPRESS			
Platform	Due	Status	Next stop
Campus Placement	After college	On-time	Patni Computers

"*I started my career with Patni Computers as a JAVA developer in 2002. Within two years of joining the organization, I got an opportunity to work in London as an onsite-coordinator managing the offshore development team in India.*"

Parna's career was like an express train full on throttle. In London, she was on the fast track - professionally. She skilfully coordinated onshore and offshore teams, keeping communication running smoothly. But eventually, personal reasons prompted her to reroute. Her career train was about to take the next turn. Was she aware of it?

TRAIN NAME - CAREER EXPRESS			
Platform	Due	Status	Next stop
Family life	After Marriage	On-time	Melbourne, Australia

"*I got married in 2007 and moved to Melbourne, Australia where I immediately got a new job as a Senior Developer. Within a year, I had my first child and thought of taking a short parenting break in my career. This break got prolonged as I became a mother again. Being a hands-on mom of two lovely sons meant, I could not have a fulltime job.*"

Life is like a long train journey with a single occurring or combination of unexpected stops and starts, long waits for a clear signal and probable diversions along the way. When you gain speed in pursuing education, career, and relationships, you feel like the train is running smoothly down the track of your dreams. Then parenthood arrives, and you pull the brake and step into the yard of parenting. This stopover is filled with joy, chaos, and sleepless nights. You wouldn't trade it for the world, yet part of you yearns for more. You don't expect an express train to be halted for long. Do you?

While she stepped aside, the IT express continued barrelling ahead. Now she pondered over her next destination, unwilling to remain stationary. What tracks would she travel down next?

TRAIN NAME - CAREER EXPRESS			
Platform	Due	Status	Next stop
Parenting	Soon	Delayed	Unknown

It's the paradox of time that when you're not looking, it speeds past in a blur. She tried multiple times to end the career break but it became difficult as time passed by. Before Parna knew it, twelve years had flown by. The IT industry evolves rapidly, and staying on the cutting edge requires conscious learning efforts. You take a break, and the knowledge gap widens, potentially derailing confidence. Like most parents, her kids were the priority, and she was content to delay her return to the field. But how is she going to come back to IT?

Life's journey is full of unexpected twists and turns that defy our plans and predictions. Soon her life came to a screeching halt, like somebody had pulled the emergency brake on a train with all the might.

"People who know me well are aware that I had a very rough personal patch and I had to get back on my feet literally overnight. Now getting into a job became a necessity rather than a choice. Also, starting back in IT after such a huge career gap was almost impossible."

TRAIN NAME - CAREER EXPRESS			
Platform	Due	Status	Next stop
Turbulent Time	Never	Derailed	Unknown

She had to pack her bags, and return to Mumbai with her two young children. Pages were flying off the calendar. Parna felt immense pressure to rebuild a stable income and life for her family, but re-entering technology with a dated resume seemed impossibly daunting.

"I was clueless about the aspects of starting my career journey again. The idea of returning into a workforce seemed very slim, especially in India, where even a gap of 6 months is frowned upon by recruiters. I had to readjust in the bustling Mumbai life, and had to support my children too, who were finding this adjustment difficult."

She checked job openings on various online portals, and the required skills column seemed written in an alien language to her.

Microservices, Docker, Kubernetes, DevOps these concepts seemed strange to her. The more she explored she realized that there was a mountain of new information, which she did not know. When a few leads at the beginning of her job search didn't materialize, she felt a bit demoralized. She felt as if the train schedule display just froze and it would become a permanent status.

TRAIN NAME - CAREER EXPRESS			
Platform	Due	Status	Next stop
Turbulent Time	Never	Derailed	Unknown

"*I was aware that there was no quick fix or simple trick to make it all go away. I was confident that employment gaps did not define me. A setback is just a setback. I had to learn to deal with probing questions about my career-break and move on to better things.*"

While she was trying to contain her inner battles, a battle raged outside in the world too. The pandemic hit the entire world and created a havoc. Covid-19 disrupted the business ecosystem globally and the job market came to a stalemate. But amidst the disruption came opportunities for remote work offering - the flexibility she needed.

As the schools were also closed for a long length of time, parents were finding it difficult to keep their kids engaged in a positive track. As a result, India had suddenly seen a rise in remote learning classes to teach kids a variety of topics. The one that was most popular among parents was teaching their kids computer programming. After all, which Indian parent wouldn't want their kid to be the next Sundar Pichai, or Satya Nadella?

"*I knew my programming skills were outdated and that I really needed to upskill to match the competition in the market. But thankfully at that time, a lot of education technology companies were coming up with online coding programs for children. During pandemic, these start-ups were scaling up as parents were enrolling their children into these online classes more. I thought I should try applying into these companies and guess what? I got a part-time role as a coding instructor!*"

Like a train resuming motion after being side-tracked for long, Parna was gaining momentum, ready to chart a new course and pick up speed. Where once she had been idling in the yard, now she was fuelled by renewed passion and purpose, engines churning to propel her dreams ahead. Now, with the unstoppable drive of a locomotive steaming uphill, Parna pushed to break out of the stalled station of her past.

TRAIN NAME - CAREER EXPRESS			
Platform	Due	Status	Next stop
A new beginning	Now	Just started	A better career

As a coding instructor, she worked with children across a broad spectrum of ages, from 6 year olds just starting out to 18 year olds with advanced skills. Her classes aimed to make programming accessible and engaging to students at all levels. She honed her skills, stretched herself for additional assignments and finally landed a full-time job with one of the fastest growing Ed-tech company in India WhiteHat Jr. which was later acquired by Byjus.

"*The job was going really well. But I wanted to continue learning and upskilling. So, I was proactively scouting for opportunities for returners. During this time, I applied and got short-listed for a fully paid scholarship from Jobsforher[1] for a Simplilearn online bootcamp to complete Masters in full stack development.*"

"*It was during this program that I got introduced to AWS. In the Simplilearn platform, there was a lab environment where we had to deploy the applications we were building. I knew that I was deploying it on AWS but the course did not cover it in depth. I was curious to know what was actually happening behind the scenes. More importantly, what is the cloud made of?*"

She continued to learn and network with people in the industry and started exploring more cloud career options for her. This led her to join communities like AspireForHer[2] and SheDares[3].

"*Joining these communities helped me understand the sought-after skills and IT trends in the industry. That is where my awakening started and I discovered all these free online webinars. I attended AWS Cloud Practitioner Essentials and AWS Technical Essentials trainings multiple times for two reasons - first, I wanted to understand*

---

[1] https://www.jobsforher.com/

[2] https://aspireforher.com/

[3] https://www.thedreamcollective.com.au/programs/she-dares/

the concepts properly and second I wanted to ensure that the cloud interests me and is something I will enjoy doing long term."

Parna wanted to sponge more knowledge. She proactively attended many such webinars after which she finally started understanding as to where her interests lie and which fields had growth potential. She understood the need to focus on technologies beyond just development and coding. Based on the industry trends, she knew she had to choose between AI/ML, Data Science or Cloud computing. She realized her interest resonates with cloud computing so she started doubling down on learning AWS.

"Google is everybody's best friend so I started Googling and discovered AWS has so many free learning opportunities."

And that's how she came across a cohort program for women all across the world called CloudUp for Her (https://pages.awscloud.com/cloudup-for-her-cloud-practitioner.html) by AWS. It helped her connect with like-minded individuals globally who were on the same path.

"This program helped me achieve AWS Certified Cloud Practitioner certification and that motivated me to keep up my learning. I would not go a day without reading an AWS news blog[1], or studying service

> 💡 *First, I wanted to understand the concepts properly and second I wanted to ensure that the cloud interests me and is something I will enjoy doing long term.*

---

[1] https://aws.amazon.com/blogs/aws/

document or doing hands-on on AWS. I also started following a lot of tech evangelists which I would recommend everybody to do so on LinkedIn."

Parna realized that increasing her network on LinkedIn could help her in more ways than she could think of. She started connecting with people in the cloud industry on LinkedIn and shared her learning journey publicly on LinkedIn.

"Initially I used LinkedIn to learn from the journey of other people, who have taken similar paths previously. Slowly I started sharing my learnings and the encouragement I got from the LinkedIn community was invaluable. I also formed a small study circle with women on a similar journey and shared tech insights daily in the group."

Through LinkedIn, Parna also got to know about BeSA (Become a Solutions Architect) program[1], a free mentoring initiative co-founded by few AWS employees. The 12-week unique mentoring program focuses on both technical and behavioural skills helping individuals to start and excel in their cloud career journey as a Solutions Architect.

"I never missed a single BeSA session. The sessions helped me to fill my gaps and achieve the AWS Certified Solutions Architect Associate certification. The BeSA team kept us motivated every week to learn more and to also share our learnings with the community."

> I started sharing my learnings and the encouragement I got from the LinkedIn community was invaluable.

---

[1]https://become-a-solutions-architect.github.io/

TRAIN NAME - CAREER EXPRESS			
Platform	Due	Status	Next stop
Become a Solutions Architect (BeSA)	Every Saturday	Actively Enrolled	Technical and Behavioural Skills

She continued learning AWS and applied for AWS SheBuilds Mentorship program. To her surprise, she got short-listed in top 50 women world-wide for this AWS flag-ship program for women from various backgrounds.

"*I never thought I would get selected. At an age when I should be the mentor, I was applying to be a mentee. This negative thought kept trying to pull me back but I managed to push it aside and go for it anyways. And I am so glad I overcame that feeling as it reaped benefits in multi-folds.*"

But success doesn't come easy. Does it?

Even after all the hard work and non-stop learning, Parna was not able to break into cloud-based roles. She did not have any experience working with cloud and the long career gap also stood out on her resume and hence she was not getting shortlisted for the roles she was hoping for.

"*I remember applying for Cloud-based jobs in multiple companies but my resume did not get shortlisted. Two companies offered me roles and one of them was a renowned global company. But both the roles were not on cloud and did not a have a long promising shelf life either. I actually had to take the tough decision of turning those roles down as I was clear in my mind that I need a role that will give me hands-on experience with AWS."*

TRAIN NAME - CAREER EXPRESS			
Platform	Due	Status	Next stop
Applying for jobs	Now	Waiting	AWS Cloud based role

Parna's perseverance and patience finally paid off when she got offers to become a technical trainer to teach AWS to other learners. She received multiple offers, including to teach AWS re/Start[1] cohorts. AWS re/Start is a free, full-time, classroom-based skills development and training program preparing unemployed or underemployed individuals to launch careers in the Cloud.

"I paid attention to the feedback I received from my mentors on why my resume was not getting shortlisted. It was mainly because my recent experience was in teaching. I thought to allow myself to play with my strengths. I should be using my teaching skills to teach AWS. Some women on the CloudUp for Her and SheDares program used to comment that I have a knack for explaining technical concepts really well. This got me thinking about my strengths. And that's how I landed with training roles at multiple companies that offered AWS trainings."

Next goal she had set for herself was to join AWS. She now had many people in her network who were willing to refer her at AWS.

---

[1] https://aws.amazon.com/training/restart/

"*I had got myself referred to AWS couple of times earlier for Solutions Architect role but my resume did not get shortlisted. So, when I got an offer to train a re/Start cohort, I got ambitious and asked for a referral for the role of Technical Trainer at AWS.*"

Parna was now leveraging all the network she had built over the time to find the right role within AWS and getting a referral. This time her resume got shortlisted and marked the beginning of her AWS interview process.

"*When my resume got shortlisted, I was thrilled and nervous at the same time. I contacted Ashish Prajapati for help. I thought to myself that there was no one better than him to help me prepare for a Technical Trainer role as he himself is a Technical Trainer at AWS.*"

Parna excelled the first round, which was a technical round. Parna had prepped for the technical phone screen so well that even the interviewer could not help but compliment her. The second round was a business case presentation.

"*Second round was tough. Interviewers thoroughly assessed both my presentation skills and my technical capabilities. I did not know the answers of few questions and I was candid about that. I told interviewers that I will have to look it up and they were fine with it. I had noted down those questions replied back to interviewers with the answers within the next 24 hours.*"

Parna got through the second round too. Next stage was famous Amazon loop which comprises usually of 5 interviews that tests candidates mostly on the Amazon Leadership Principles (LPs)[1]

"For my loop interview preparation, I created a spreadsheet for every LP and I tried to think of at least two scenarios in my past where I would have demonstrated that. This is where behavioural track sessions of BeSA helped me most along with the other videos on YouTube."

Parna left no station behind during her journey preparing for the loop. Letting no obstacle or downtime slow her acceleration, she stoked her engines with determination. She connected with few people in Amazon to get clarity about a few LPs and mapped her stories to align with the LPs.

"I had very limited recent work experience being a restarter so I had to customize or recycle my stories to fit in certain LPs. Few of my stories were not about the work experience. They were about the time I was on career break."

After every loop interview, Parna used to strike out the stories she had used in order to keep the repeats to a minimum and doubled down on the other stories she prepared for next interview.

"I remember my last interview of the loop got re-scheduled

> After every loop interview, Parna used to strike out the stories she had used in order to keep the repeats to a minimum and doubled down on the other stories she prepared for next interview.

---

[1] https://www.amazon.jobs/en/principles

and delayed by more than a week because the interviewer was not available. With such long wait times sometimes you feel like giving up as the end seems so far away. But I knew that I had to still perform the best irrespective as the last person could have been the bar raiser[1] so couldn't take any chances and couldn't let my guard down either."

The full hiring journey lasted three long months. Parna's pulse raced as she opened the recruiter's email after the final interview stop. She was thrilled when she saw the email of Job offer from AWS. She beamed brighter than locomotive headlights, like a kid embarking on a Christmas morning train ride. Her dream destination had arrived at last.

TRAIN NAME - CAREER EXPRESS			
Platform	Due	Status	Next stop
AWS Technical Trainer	Now	Arrived	A soaring career

Ask Parna on how she feels to be part of AWS

"Surreal" she says.

"There were times in my life I felt I wouldn't make it back to the industry. But, having cracked a known-to-be-tough interview process and now, belong to one of the most reputed organizations is indeed surreal, several times so. As many say, hard work does pays off, also

---

[1] https://www.aboutamazon.co.uk/news/working-at-amazon/what-is-a-bar-raiser-at-amazon

networking. But, my journey to further upskill has not stopped. I know I will be working with extremely smart people and that I will have to learn to keep up the pace but I'm thrilled. I look forward to growing my career in AWS over and beyond."

. . .

Learning has become an unrelenting fixation for Parna that she cannot relinquish. As a technical trainer, she assists AWS customers in comprehending and mastering cloud services. This occupation nourishes her hunger for knowledge, as she must continually absorb the latest advancements to address inquiries posed in the classroom.

She is now contributing back to the community and empowering others by mentoring CloudUp for Her cohorts. She is also an active volunteer of the BeSA program, that played a vital role in getting her not just into AWS as a technology but the company itself. You could find her delivering technical sessions, answering questions, and interviewing guests as part of the BeSA program. Over time, Parna has observed her own evolution from mentee to mentor, from novice to expert.

She reminds us that a career gap isn't a red flag. Either you decided to take a career break, or other uncontrollable factors decided it for you. If there's a gap in your work history, it shouldn't mean that you're never going to step back into your industry again. It marks a time in your life where you could have learned new skills, adjusted your career path, spent more time with your family, or taken better care of your health. By no means is it something to hide.

Parna shows that by learning from detours and believing in yourself, you can complete any journey undefeated. She wants others to know that career breaks do not have to be permanent - as long as you sustain your engine, you can restart your train again in time. Parna encourages to use the pause to keep developing skills, preparing for re-entry when ready.

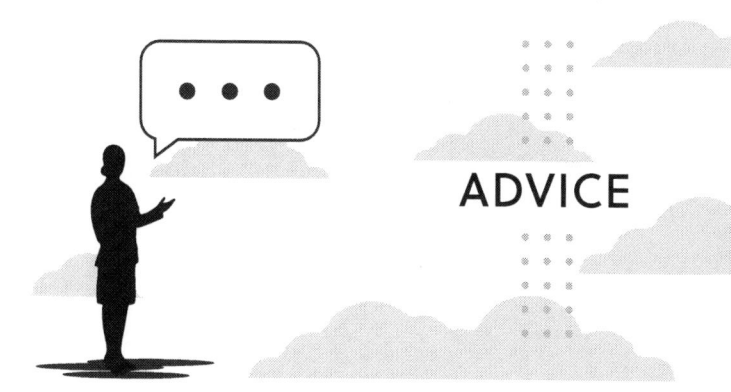

Advice when following a Cloud career path

- **Build a habit of learning** - Be consistent in your learning, maybe even 30 minutes a day. It ultimately becomes a habit with long term benefits.

- **Stay up to date** - Keep up with latest tech to increase your shelf life. Leverage the internet for learning opportunities and mentorship openings.

- **Combine theory with practice** - Do hands-on for concept clarity and retention, theoretical knowledge will not take you very far without practice.

ACTION

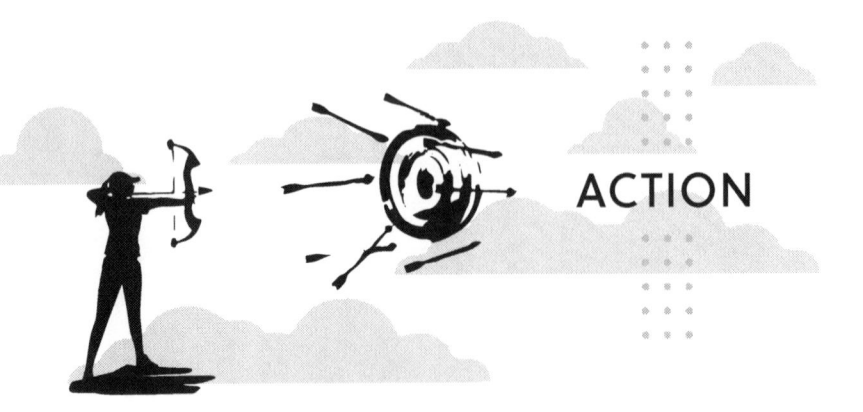

Actions to take that will drive meaningful progress

- **Network well** - Consciously network with people who will advocate for you or add to your knowledge

- **Be part of community** - Interact- and engage with communities other than your workplace. Read and share tech blogs and articles on a daily basis

- **Build your digital presence** - Re-vamp your LinkedIn profile as that's your digital identity and people who don't know or wish to know you professionally make opinions based on that

ALERT

Alerts to avoid common pitfalls that can hinder success

- **Don't doubt** - Never underestimate your capabilities based on your status today. Do not be swayed by detractors. No one knows you more than you.

- **Don't travel alone** - Reach out for help, don't pretend you are a one-person army. It's unbelievable how many people are ready to support you on your journey.

- **Age is just a number** - Don't let your age stop you from achieving your goals

The Progressives

Used prior IT knowledge as stepping stones to Cloud

With robust technical skills and determined ambition, these climbers conquered fresh trails to become lead guides in the Clouds. Their journeys show how foundational IT skills can pave upward paths to Cloud career peaks.

The Progressives

The Progressives

Kesha Williams
Cloud & AI Leader,
AWS Machine Learning Hero

07 Once Coding Java Applications,
    Now Decoding Machine Learning in Cloud

Sammy Cheung
AWS Ambassador,
Champion AWS Authorized Instructor

08 Trained Body for Ultra Marathons,
    Trained Mind for Cloud Certifications

Lucy Wang
Founder,
Tech with Lucy

09 From Internship at AWS,
    To Cloud Career Influencer

Progressives

Once Coding Java Applications, Now Decoding Machine Learning in Cloud

07

Kesha Williams

Cloud & AI Leader,
AWS Machine Learning Hero

If you have ever studied any computer programming language, you would know about infinite loops (or endless loops). If executed, infinite loops normally cause the entire system to become unresponsive.

What if there is an infinite loop that we need to include in our life? Would it not crash our system?

While growing up in Monks Corner, a small family-oriented town in South Carolina, Kesha was surrounded by a loving family, cousins, brothers, and sisters.

"The closest movie theatres, malls, and nice restaurants were about 45-minutes away in the well-known city of Charleston, most of my aunts, uncles, and cousins were close by. That means my younger sister and I, would always get together with our cousins to celebrate holidays and birthdays. Like clockwork we saw each other most Sundays at church."

As she was growing up, she saw her mother managing the balancing act between job and family like a practiced performer. Her mother was working full time and with every step on the ladder of success she climbed, Kesha felt it's not an "either-or" choice between career or family, but it is an "and" choice. Her father had a degree in Chemistry and initially worked for well-known chemical manufacturers across the US. He was often seen in a white lab coat creating formulas for everyday household products. Gradually his white attire got exchanged with a sharp suit as he ascended through his career journey and became an Executive VP.

"*My parents are my inspiration, they had ensured that my sister and I got the love and warmth of the family, but they also ensured that we were not soaring unchecked. They were strict, and sometimes I wasn't permitted to do things typical teenagers were allowed to do. This somehow rooted a yearning for independence in me. To this day, I do not like being told what to do and often clash with authoritarian leadership styles when someone dictates their terms to me.*"

Kesha initially wanted to be a teacher as she enjoyed helping others and showing them the "right" way to do things. But her father told her that she would never make any money being a teacher. After that conversation, she had put aside her career goal of becoming a teacher. If not a teacher, what else?

Kesha's towering dreams could not get a foothold in a small town; she needed a bigger stage. At the age of 17, she left for the "big" city of Atlanta, Georgia. She attended Spelman College, and selected Computer Science and Mathematics. Her choice of subjects was majorly influenced by the "computer-as-a-toy" model.

"*I was exposed to computers when I was a teenager in high school. My father purchased a personal computer from the local Radio Shack to do the family finances. He placed the computer in a room that played a dual role as both his office and my playroom. I had a Barbie doll in one hand and a computer manual in the other hand. I saw the computer as just another toy and I would spend hours "playing" on it. I didn't realize until much later that what I called "playing-on-the-computer" was actually writing computer programs in the BASIC programming language."

During the summer of her junior year in high school, she was enrolled in a summer science enrichment program at a local college that focused on Computer Science and Chemistry. It was a several week-long program and imparted college-level courses. This experience was instrumental in cementing her love and passion for technology. She realized that this "playing-on-the-computer" could be her career choice too, and she could do it for the whole life. The loops, statements, variables, functions became the new Lego blocks that helped her build a ladder to success.

That early introduction to computers set her up for a lifelong pursuit of technology and a love for building and creating. So, an academically brilliant girl, with a bit of computer knowledge, and passion to pursue computers as a subject for studies should be acing the computer classes in her college. Right?

"It was HARD! I just remember being stuck in the computer lab every weekend trying to get my code to compile while my friends were out partying! Computer Science was a challenge at first, I actually withdrew from my first programming class (on Pascal) because I was going to fail it. At that point, my father gave me an ultimatum to change my major to something else because he thought my withdrawing showed that I couldn't succeed in Computer Science."

It seemed Kesha's 'Hello world' program was getting stuck in an infinite loop. She needed to make it run without any errors.

After her father's insistence, Kesha considered other majors like Chemistry or Political Science, but none of them inspired as much passion in her as technology. It was a "fight or flight" situation. Quitting didn't align with Kesha's indomitable spirit, and she was not ready to surrender. Kesha chose to soar, not settle. She patched her tech knowledge gaps with relentless grit. Hour after hour, she honed her coding skills in the computer lab, reviewing documentation until the wee hours. Kesha's passion for computers was an internal flame she chose to stoke, not extinguish.

It was a voluntary torture and that may have made no sense at all to a rational mind. Against her father's advice, she stuck to the selected major of Computer Science and went on to graduate with honors. Along the way she earned an academic scholarship. Hard work fuelled her persistence through each obstacle on her path to success. Later she earned an M.S. in Information Systems from the University of Phoenix. Kesha allowed no roadblock to deter her from pursuing her dreams. Compilation successful without any errors!

```
System.out.println("I won't give up.");
```

Onward to the next program.

"My first technology job was with the National Security Agency

(NSA). I held a top-secret security clearance. I absolutely loved the technology I worked with at the NSA as an intern—the job showed me that I made the right career choice. It also opened my eyes to what it means to be underrepresented in tech. I was the only African American person on the team and there was only one other woman."

"On my last day of internship, I remember stopping by the other woman's cubicle to give her my well wishes. She told me that she knew I would succeed in tech because I was tall. Yes, she actually said tall! I was flabbergasted! I remember thinking to myself, "what about my brain". That was appalling, and it showed me that a woman in tech could be judged on something other than her brain!"

This colleague did an unexpected favor—her undermining compliment illuminated Kesha about the hidden biases women face. It revealed how women in tech are often judged on anything but merit—appearance, personality, demographics.

Earlier in her career, Kesha was often held to a different standard than her white male counterparts. She saw that men were promoted based on potential and that women –especially African American —were promoted only after they had proven over and over and over again that they could do the job at the next level.

Kesha saw others progress on a fast track while she strained for footing on a slower climb. She saw a biased and divided world where her male counterparts were given high profile projects and mentorship to help them get to the next level, while she was offered nothing and often turned down when she asked for the same level of support provided to others. Had she accepted this as a standard?

"*I'm the type of person that finds the positive in every situation. The rewarding piece is that these setbacks have given me a really strong work ethic. Those setbacks have trained me to put 110% in everything I do. In every task, going above and beyond is natural for me—it's survival. And I'm my own biggest fan – I don't need external validation from anyone, I find validation from within!*"

Despite all these roadblocks, with you-can't-stop-me attitude Kesha has reached the escape-velocity. She was not confined to a single orbit as a geo-stationary satellite. Her coding skills excelled day-by-day, she became more fluent in computer languages. Her passion for the technology and tenacity for learning took her from one job to the other. Her choice for the next role was based on a Boolean choice. Will I be learning something new in the next role?

```
if (learning_in_new_role > current_knowledge) {
    System.out.println("Accept the role");
} else {
    System.out.println("Reject the role");
}
```

"*I remember when the Java programming language came out, I was doing web development using ASP (Active Server Pages), Active X Controls, and VB Script. When I researched Java, I thought the*

> 💡 *I'm the type of person that finds the positive in every situation. The rewarding piece is that these setbacks have given me a really strong work ethic..*

language was going to take over the world, and I knew it was where I needed to take my career. I left the organization where I was working for an opportunity to learn Java on the job doing web development. And I can say that was one of the best career decisions I've ever made."

Her desire to learn Java was intense, she soon understood the complicated details of a modern programming language. While she was learning Java, she started explaining these intricacies to others and absolutely enjoyed it. Her mentor saw latent talents within her that she herself had not yet realized and encouraged her to pursue an M.S. degree so that she could start teaching part-time. This led her to start teaching part-time in 2009 in the Java Certification program at the University of California, Irvine Extension. Without that guidance from her amazing mentor during the formative stages of her career, she would not have been where she is today.

"This part-time job helped me to dig into my childhood passion of teaching. I've come a full circle. This led me to eventually teach hundreds and thousands of learners through online learning platforms. To this day, I enjoy telling my father, "Hey Dad, I actually "can" make money being a teacher. Did you see my new online course?" I teach part-time to this day."

```
boolean isTeachingRewarding = true;
System.out.println(isTeachingRewarding); // Outputs true
```

In 2013, she was honored with the Distinguished Instructor Award by the University of California, Irvine Extension. This award recognized instructors whose contributions helped the university stay at the forefront of education and empower students with career-advancing skills. It acknowledged her dedication to providing top-tier instruction and enrichment to learners. Shortly after receiving this distinction, she was invited to join the Java Program Advisory Committee. She accepted and served on the committee until 2019.

At times in her career, she found herself pigeonholed in support roles - fixing bugs and tweaking existing Java apps. The roles didn't give her the opportunity to expand her skills. Undeterred, Kesha devoted her personal time to mastering advanced Java. She knew upskilling was her ladder to escape the humdrum of the role. After upskilling, she took that knowledge back to the organization to help them become more efficient and find better ways of coding and supporting solutions.

"I also then started sharing my knowledge with others, outside of the organization, by teaching and speaking at conferences. Sharing my expertise outside work boosted my reputation everywhere. It made me look valuable to my company. This helped me to climb the career ladder and move into engineering leadership roles. My outside teaching really grew my career."

Kesha climbed the corporate ladder steadily. She started managing a team of Java Engineers and contractors developing custom solutions that ran on-premises. The organization she was working for steered

> 💡 She knew upskilling was her ladder to escape the humdrum of the role.

towards its first Cloud migration in 2014, and her team was entrusted for refactoring the on-premises monoliths to a serverless architecture running on AWS infrastructure. This was the first time she was exploring the potential of the Cloud.

"I remember the excitement I felt when the Java programming was released. I thought the Java language was going to take over the world – and I was right! The same excitement I felt for Java back then, I feel for the Cloud. The Cloud is taking over the world, and I want to be a part of that innovation! If this Cloud thing doesn't work out though, I can always go back and sling some Java code!"

Kesha was not new in learning-the-next-big-thing. Her Cloud learning journey was ignited by her catch phrase - *"learn as you build"*. At first, most of her Cloud learning was self-taught. She learnt best by picking up a fun app idea and then tried to build it using AWS. During the process of building, she learned how each service worked and strengthened her knowledge of the Cloud.

```
while ("I do not master Cloud") {
    System.out.println("Keep Learning");
}
```

Like so many others, she learned through the A Cloud Guru platform, Ryan Kroonenburg becoming her first Cloud teacher. Years later, she came full circle to join the A Cloud Guru team in 2019. She powered their mission to "teach the Cloud to the world" as a Principal AWS Training Architect. Whether at work or in her personal pursuits, the Cloud infused her days with discovery and growth. She immersed herself in AWS ever-expanding universe, continuously learning and reaching new heights.

"*Outside of work, I started "playing" around with developing Alexa Skills, which is backed by services like AWS Lambda, Amazon DynamoDB, Amazon S3, and more. I was one of the first developers to test the ASK SDK for Java and provide feedback to the AWS development team. Alexa Skills development really strengthened my knowledge of the Cloud.*"

While soaring in the Cloud she also achieved AWS Certified Cloud Practitioner certification. Kesha knew the importance of certifications as probably they prove someone's capability and knowledge. It also validates that you know how things are supposed to work. However, she strongly believed that certifications alone aren't enough to prove that you can actually do the work, that's why having an online portfolio of projects is important too. She later achieved AWS Certified Alexa Skill Builder Specialty and AWS Certified Machine Learning Specialty. She found Alexa and ML Speciality certifications, were more aligned to her aspirations and programming skill. *From a practitioner to a specialist. Remarkable.*

The other spectrum of her Cloud journey was to transition her Java skills to Machine Learning. She used the Amazon Machine Learning (i.e., the precursor to Amazon SageMaker) service to build a crime prediction model that she modelled after the concept of pre-crime from the movie *Minority Report*. This was pretty novel – perfect example of creativity and intelligence. Though she never looked for recognition from outside to validate her work, but this was a significant point of her journey.

"*I won numerous awards, earned several award nominations, and authored several courses and conference talks on my crime predicting model that I named SAM (Suspicious Activity Monitor). I even won a spot on the TED stage to talk about how machine learning can remove bias in policing as a part of their Spotlight Presentation Academy. My superpower is combining machine learning and the Cloud!*"

```
String technology = "Machine Learning ";
String location = "on Cloud";
String my_superpower = technology.concat(location);
System.out.println(my_superpower);
```

And this was just the beginning. She started giving back to the community by mentoring others through formal programs like WEST (Women Entering and Staying in Tech)[1] and WWC[2]. She also travelled the world speaking at tech conferences sharing her lessons learned on topics like AWS/Cloud, machine learning, and Java. When you turn your passion to help uplift others, recognition comes as a by-product.

"*As I was so excited about how "easy" AWS made machine learning that I started telling everyone. I would speak at local meetups, write blog posts, teach workshops, author online courses, and travel the world speaking at tech conferences about it. I came on the radar of someone on the machine learning team at AWS because of my evangelism in the community. I was nominated to become an AWS Machine Learning Hero[3] in 2019, and got accepted to the program.*"

---

[1] https://www.joinwest.org/

[2] https://www.womenwhocode.com/

[3] https://aws.amazon.com/developer/community/heroes/

```
String consistent = "sharing actively in the community";
if ("sharing actively in the community".equals(consistent)) {
    AWS Hero;
}
```

Kesha had perfectly coalesced her passion for computer and teaching in various shapes and forms. Networking and building your brand are as important as having a continuous learning mindset. She is a frequent guest on industry-leading podcasts and often write technical blog posts for sites like InfoQ, the AWS blog, A Cloud Guru blog, and more.

"*I stay up to date by continuing to "learn as I build". At night, once everyone is in bed, I'm always up on my computer, building and learning. I love to innovate with technology. For me, "playing on the computer" never gets old – I've been doing it since being a teenager! And after I build something new using the latest and greatest technology, I share my lessons learned through either speaking at a tech conference or authoring an online course on the subject.*"

She feeds her creative side by innovating and using technology in fun ways. Her latest fun project used AWS DeepLens to build a soda-theft detection system to stop her kids from taking soda out of the refrigerator without asking.

> 💡 Networking and building your brand are as important as having a continuous learning mindset.

She participated in the "largest code debugging/bug fixing competition" on 12/2/21 at AWS re:Invent. This event was recognized by Guinness Book as a record where 613 developers worked together to fix the bugs.

Kesha plans to continue *learning by doing*. She remains committed in sharing her knowledge to help others grow. Through tireless hands-on practice, she masters abilities that she passes on to guide others' development. The cycle recurs - each lesson learned is then shared, her widening expertise reaching far beyond herself. Kesha sees life as an infinite learning journey. This is one of the loops she doesn't want to break.

```
public void an-infinite-loop () {
    do {
        Learn();
        Share();
    } while (alive);
}
```

Sometimes Infinite loops are needed.

This journey has no end, the learning never stops, and Kesha is passionate to bring as many as possible along for the ride.

Advice when following a Cloud career path

- **No break condition** - Never stop learning! The Cloud changes at a rapid rate, and you'll need to work hard to keep your skills current!

- **Front-end** - Networking and building your brand are as important as having a continuous learning mindset. Build your network by sharing your learning with others.

- **Recursion** - Find validation from within - Don't let how others treat you make you question your own abilities.

ACTION

Actions to take that will drive meaningful progress

- **Learn by teaching** - Learn a new topic like you're going to have to teach it to someone else. When you approach learning like this, you go far beyond surface-level knowledge.

- **Learn by doing** - Don't be afraid to be hands-on with technology when you're just starting out. Hands-on exercises help to solidify your knowledge.

- **Learn by sharing** - Document your learning, speak at local meetups, write blog posts, conduct workshops, author online courses. Remember the more you share, the more you learn.

ALERT

Alerts to avoid common pitfalls that can hinder success

- **Not having Growth Mindset** - Just accept the fact that you've signed up for a career of lifelong learning! The sooner you accept that and dedicate your life to continuous learning, the better off you'll be.

- **Trying to rush the learning process** - Learning the Cloud is a journey that doesn't happen overnight. You may be working with technology for years, but focus on learning something new every day.

- **Focusing solely on earning certifications** - Certifications help but are only a small part of the learning journey. It's important to have hands-on experience with designing and building Cloud-native applications.

Pathfinders | Undefeated | **Progressives** | Liberators | Accelerators | Pinnacles

Trained Body for Ultra Marathons, Trained Mind for Cloud Certifications

08

Sammy Cheung

AWS Ambassador,
Champion AWS Authorized Instructor

Running a marathon is an experience that profoundly challenges and transforms participants. It requires endurance, grit, and the ability to push past discomfort and pain. The person who lines up at the start is fundamentally different from the one who crosses the finish line.

Does this hold true for a Cloud Ultramarathon too?

At the tender age of 5, Sammy was finding it hard to adjust to the bustling city of Hong Kong. In 1975 his family migrated from Bao Tou, China, where Mandarin was spoken, to Hong Kong, where the day-to-day language was Cantonese. Another dimension of this language struggle was English, which was the main medium of teaching in school.

His father worked as a lecturer of Electrical and Electronic Engineering (E&E) at Hong Kong polytechnic. His mother was a university graduate but decided to be a homemaker after their relocation to Hong Kong. Most of the time kids are excited about going to a new place, but for Sammy, this experience was not so polished. Sammy struggled with studies early in school due to linguistic barriers.

"*When I took my first mathematics exam, I scored 4 out of 100. At that moment I thought, maybe I'm dumb. Those days, failing an exam meant receiving a physical punishment from the teacher. I used to get lot of punishments.*"

Like a typical kid, Sammy enjoyed playing video games more than studying and it made him realize that he was more of an audio-visual learner.

"*The first time I used computers for games at age of 7. My father tried to teach me programming on Texas Instrument TiI-99. He gave up after numerous attempts, as my only interest was solving the games' visual challenges. I learn 10 times faster watching videos or listening to voice notes rather than reading a textbook.*"

He realized that mathematics or any other subject was never the problem, the problem was the theoretical approach in the school. Some teachers realized this and encouraged him to learn through critical thinking, and asked him to focus on why things work that way and for what purpose. Sammy leaned on to his visual learning abilities and surprised everyone in the 5th year of his elementary school when he achieved top 10 ranking in his grade's mathematics competition. He naturally got inclined more towards computers and preferred spending time toying with it instead of reading books.

Initially Sammy doubted his ability and did not plan to study in college as he foresaw himself failing to get a degree. He later realized that there was no harm in trying and at the age of 19, he moved to US to pursue computer science engineering, at California State University. Were his doubts real?

"*I did not do well in college. I had to work part time to support myself by studying abroad. I did not have much time to have fun as I was always between classes, work, and more classes. On the weekends I had to work as a waiter, sometimes the whole day. It was my interest in computer science and programming that kept me afloat and empowered me to finish my degree.*"

After completing his graduation, he landed his first job in 1993 as a System programmer. He built custom debugger for application developer using C and Assembly language. This was a perfect job for him, as he was more comfortable talking to computers than people. Solving a technical problem is easy when compared with solving people issue. Isn't it?

"*I loved the job. The best part was that I didn't have to meet lot of people or answer any calls while I was programming. By this time, I thoroughly loved and enjoyed coding. I used to work in front of the computer continuously isolating myself from the outside world.*"

After his initial stint as a programmer, he started working with databases and became a seasoned Database Developer and then Database Administrator. For over two decades he stayed into a linear career ladder, and eventually became a Database Architect. While being complacent he never ignored the opportunity to learn and grow his knowledge. He also started observing a specific trend in his company and the industry.

"*My interaction with Cloud started in 2017. I realized there were two parallel universes altogether in my company - a Cloud team and a non-Cloud team. The Cloud team was making more money than *the non-Cloud team and they got to work on the latest technologies. I fell into the category of a non-Cloud team and we used to work on maintaining existing legacy systems. I wanted to make the switch to the other side and it was that urge that motivated me to learn the Cloud."*

But it is never easy to start learning something completely new specially if you do not have any project to work on. He tried approaching few people in the company for Cloud specific roles but did not get any as he lacked knowledge of AWS. Nobody wanted to trust a newbie with production systems. Would you?

Instead of waiting for the opportunity to come, Sammy left the company's non-Cloud team and joined another company that was committed to Cloud technology and who trusted Sammy could upskill quickly on AWS.

Sammy leaned on his runner spirit. He had been an active ultra-marathon runner for a long time. Before any long-distance race, he knew a warm-up was an important part of preparation that people often neglected. For a runner, this could be walking, jogging, or easy running initially. He started his *warm-up* for the Cloud marathon. He turned to online Cloud learning platform, A Cloud Guru.

"It was difficult to get into the learning mode again after all these years. I have always been the visual learner so the video courses by Ryan Kroonenburg, co-founder of A Cloud Guru, were really helpful."

Learning without a clear goal felt directionless to Sammy, like a runner logging junk miles. In running, training without purposeful structure lacks focus. Sammy craved intentional learning, not aimless studying. So, he set his sights on an AWS certification, like a runner choosing a target race. Just as runners train with specific workouts, Sammy pursued certification with a structured learning path. Like a race bib, the exam date kicked his training into high gear. With a finish line in place, his studying had purpose.

"*I started with AWS Certified Solution Architect Associate certification and frankly I found it difficult to grasp all the concepts initially. I wish someone would have guided me to start with AWS Certified Cloud practitioner first. It is always better to run 1 mile before running 10 miles. But starting with the difficult one worked well for me as the second certification was relatively easier. After I got two certifications in a succession, there was no looking back - I decided to do one AWS certification every month.*"

Sammy planned his certification journey like a marathon pacing strategy - starting steady to avoid burning out. Could he maintain steady pacing for the long haul?

The three AWS Associate level certifications were his opening miles, building core Cloud skills. Then he started with AWS Specialty certifications and surged by passing AWS Certified Security Specialty Certification. But the Advanced Networking Certification exam loomed like a big, tough hill that breaks runners. Though Sammy trained hard, the difficult concepts tripped him up and he failed. His morale and motivation drained like a runner who depleted all his energy.

As an experienced marathoner, Sammy knew all about "hitting the wall" - that ominous fatigue around mile 20 when the finish seems so close yet so far. Runners' energy gets used up, legs feel weak, and reaching the end is really hard. Will he be able to cross the finish line? Or will he be a DNF (Did Not Finish) in Cloud marathon?

Distance running is mental resilience. Runners need aid stations to refresh and refuel. Also, the cheering from the crowd in the last leg works best in rejuvenating the motivation of the runners to cross the finish line. For Sammy that motivation came through an interview call from AWS. He resumed his Cloud learning journey to prepare for the AWS interview.

"*Getting an interview call from AWS helped boost my confidence, the joy came back. Even though I was not able to clear the interview, I was ready to resume my certifications journey and determined to get fully AWS Certified. I started studying and appeared for the certification exams only after I was fully prepared. I was really enjoying the knowledge I was gaining and passing certifications became secondary.*"

Learning became an obsession Sammy could not shake. Sammy's employer finally took notice of his hard work in upskilling himself. They were impressed by his initiative to get AWS certified. Management team empowered Sammy to train and mentor other members to upskill on Cloud. He continued to expand his Cloud skills by managing the AWS Infrastructure, including data tier, networking, and security. He used to regularly review the AWS cost usage and eventually lowered his employer's AWS operation costs by half in 2019.

"*I was learning at a fast pace both by working on real life projects and by continuing my AWS Certification journey. I remember getting my AWS Alexa Skill builder certification in April 2020 and becoming fully AWS certified. And in May 2020 when the covid-19 pandemic hit and mass layoffs happened, I was let go from my company.*"

It is almost impossible not to take a layoff personally especially when you have been an integral part of the company. Sammy naturally thought - "*Is this my reward for getting 12x certified?*" He started looking for the jobs but as it was the beginning of the pandemic all companies had paused hiring. He felt like the marathon was called off when he was literally half way through.

Sammy started to realize that the number of certifications, or your qualifications has nothing to do with whether you have a job or not. You can be well qualified and certified, but you may not have relevant opportunities available because of the economic conditions. This notion may make someone doubt the value of certifications at such times, but not Sammy. He in fact doubled down on certifications to embarked on his multi-Cloud journey.

"*The hiring managers were not sure about hiring me due to the uncertainties. During this time, one of the recruiters asked me if I knew Google Cloud Platform (GCP). I definitely didn't know much about it, but I took it on myself to learn since I didn't have anything to do. This is how I got introduced to GCP and embarked on my multi-Cloud journey. I fully funded myself for the course and took the exams and passed.*"

During this time, he also got a chance to become an AWS Authorised Instructor (AAI). Once you qualify and get sponsored through an AWS Learning Partner, you prepare for the instructor authorization that involves multi-day evaluation. During these sessions, wannabe instructors are evaluated on their knowledge of the official curriculum as well as their skills to deliver live and efficient training courses.

"*I utilized my time when I got laid-off to learn GCP and prepare to become AWS Authorized Instructor. It was difficult to search for jobs and also keep learning in parallel. Staying indoors full time and studying for more than 12 hours a day shifted my focus away from fitness and even my running stopped completely. But the upskilling did help me to come out of difficult times during the pandemic.*"

> 💡 You can be well qualified and certified, but you may not have relevant opportunities available because of the economic conditions.

As the saying goes - *when the going gets tough, the tough get going.* After getting laid off, Sammy became GCP certified within couple of months, got a new job within four months and became AWS Authorized Instructor within 6 months.

"*If you are certified and well qualified with proper skills, opportunity will surely come your way. Difficult times are a time for you to grow and upskill yourself. If opportunities are not knocking on your door, build another door.*"

By now, Sammy was fully AWS Certified and had multiple GCP certifications. But why did he think of getting Oracle Cloud and Microsoft Azure certifications? Wasn't it the weirdest *cross-training* regime an athlete may think of?

"*Well, Oracle Cloud was running a campaign to get people certified for free. I already had good knowledge of Cloud so I was able to get them without much effort or any monetary investment. But for Microsoft Azure, the organization I was working for needed Azure Certified employees to become an Azure Premier Partner. So, they were offering additional bonus to employees for each Azure certification they would achieve. It was an extra income and I started my streak again. One certification every month. This time I was running on the Azure track and soon I was fully certified on Azure too.*"

Sammy gained knowledge and certification across various

Difficult times are a time for you to grow and upskill yourself. If opportunities are not knocking on your door, build another door.

technologies. His thirst for knowledge took him to achieve 90+ certifications across Cloud providers and in other technologies like Kubernetes. This broad spectrum of knowledge had surely had come-in handy while designing solutions for customers. He started working as a solutions architect initially in Berg and later in Cloudticity.

"*One of the most important highlight of becoming a Solution Architect is gaining trust of the customers. Since I was well qualified and had the right information, it was easy for me to gain trust of the customers. Getting the certifications and being able to compare service choices definitely helped me provide better value to my customers.*"

Earning certifications was just a milestone - staying sharp in the shifting Cloud landscape was an endless pursuit. Like marathoners who continue training after races, Sammy maintained his Cloud fitness with ongoing learning. His *cool-down* period like that of a runner walking after a hard run, is also dotted with various certification renewals and learnings.

"*First time is always difficult, but the second time, you have to update the knowledge and add on to the foundation you have already created. I try to update myself continuously about all the major Cloud providers and I make sure to interact with the customers regularly. The daily conversations with customers and providing solutions to their business problems help me to stay up-to date. Renewing certifications happened in auto-mode.*"

Sammy's dedication to maintaining all his AWS certifications paid dividends when he joined the AWS partner Cloudreach. His up-to-date credentials led to him being named an AWS Ambassador - a recognition for influential AWS Partner employees. Most rewarding, his comprehensive certifications made Sammy eligible for the prestigious AWS Golden Jacket award.

Earning the Golden Jacket is akin to runners being awarded the Abbott Six Star Finisher Medal. This prestigious medal is only given to marathoners who complete all six World Marathon Major races. It demonstrates remarkable endurance mastery across the highest echelon of marathons. Just as the Six Star Finisher Medal recognizes comprehensive marathon excellence, the AWS Golden Jacket celebrates those who have earned every AWS certification available.

"*People ask me why get AWS Certified? The most important reason to be certified is to be equipped so that we can deliver the*

> *I try to update myself continuously about all the major Cloud providers and I make sure to interact with the customers regularly.*

promise of the Cloud to our clients. But to get the special AWS fully certified gold jacket? Priceless!"

As Sammy grew in his career, he realized networking and knowledge sharing is a very important aspect of growth. As he had seen the struggle and confusion of a new learner first hand, he started sharing his learning with wider audience through LinkedIn, Meetups and technical conferences. This selfless knowledge sharing earned him the coveted award of AWS Community Builder in March 2022. In September 2023, he received AWS Ambassador - Certification All-Star Award and got his second AWS Gold Jacket, the AWS Ambassador edition.

"One of the challenges that I faced during my initial Cloud journey was that I did not have a mentor who could guide me. Now I am trying my best to share knowledge and be a mentor to others while trying to be a game changer for business. Hope I make a small impact to people's live before I depart from this world."

. . .

Sammy had undergone quite a transformation from his early days of introverted programming interest. Through diligent skill-building, he developed into a confident Cloud professional adept at engaging with customers and learners daily.

> *People ask me why get AWS Certified? The most important reason to be certified is to be equipped so that we can deliver the promise of the Cloud to our clients.*

Guided by his motto of the 3Ls - Learn, Live, Lead - Sammy maintained a growth mindset. Like a committed marathoner, he viewed learning as an endless pursuit with no final finish line. There was always another Cloud technology frontier and certification to conquer.

While his early career steps may have been timid, he had built up the resilience and determination of a seasoned ultramarathoner. Sammy possessed the mental toughness and curiosity to go the distance on his Cloud marathon quest.

Advice when following a Cloud career path

- **Tame your mind** - Your mind will lure you to stay in the path of least resistance because its comfortable in that box. Don't live a life defined by the limits you imagine.

- **Stay fit** - Mentally and Physically - Do not compromise on physical or mental fitness in order to achieve something. Staying in front of the screen for 10 to 12 hours is mentally draining so it is important to take care of yourself throughout the journey.

- **Regroup, Rest and Reset** - When you are low it can be easy to see everything through a prism of negativity. In those moments, regroup your resources, think through the situation and reset your journey. Quitting is tempting but doesn't win the race.

ACTION

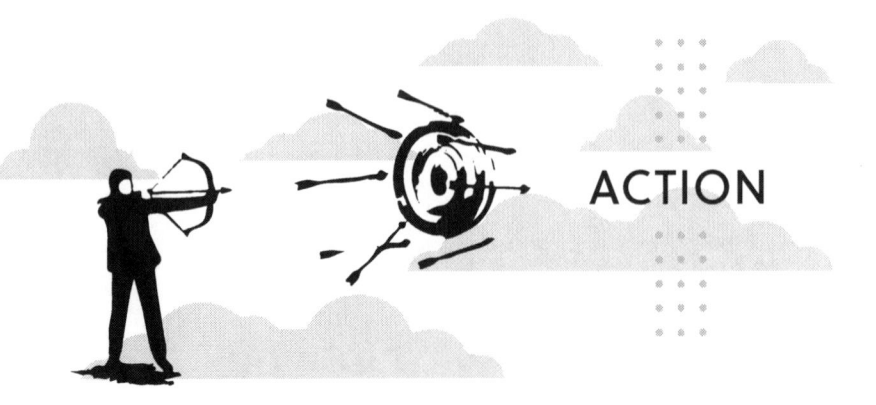

Actions to take that will drive meaningful progress

- **Take that step** - Whether you have to run a 100m sprint or a 26.2-mile marathon you have to take first step. Figure out what type of learning works well for you and get started.

- **Adjust your pace** - It may not be possible to run at the same pace for each split. Speed up going through the topics that are easy, known to you and devote more time in complex and unknown topics.

- **Share knowledge** - Knowledge is the only thing in the world which increases as you share. However small, share your learnings, you will be enriching yourself and others.

ALERT

Alerts to avoid common pitfalls that can hinder success

- **Avoid unstructured learning** - Randomly going through a learning topic or frequently changing your learning resource will lead to waste of time and efforts. Structure your learning journey carefully.

- **Don't be afraid of failure** - No one ever starts walking (forget running) without falling down. Don't let fear of failure callous your mind. Fears and doubts are normal, and you're going to figure it out.

- **Don't stay still** - If you are not moving forward, you have already starting moving backward. Technology evolves whether you like it or not. Don't stop your learning regime.

Pathfinders   Undefeated   **Progressives**   Liberators   Accelerators   Pinnacles

From Internship at AWS, To Cloud Career Influencer

09

Lucy Wang
Founder,
Tech with Lucy

If you are an expert chef, no matter how skillful, cooking for yourself is not good; the joy is cooking for others. It's the same with knowledge. Hoarding knowledge to oneself never results in growth, but if you share it, it multiplies.

Let's hear the story of the chef who is open to sharing her secret recipe.

What is your precious memory when you were at the age of 13? For Lucy, it is setting up an e-commerce store selling small keychain collectibles (or 'squishies'). She was getting her early lessons in generating sales, packing orders, and connecting with customers worldwide. Not sure if she understood the meaning of the word entrepreneur at that time, but she was definitely one. This early adventure of hers was possible because of encouragement from her parents, who were her biggest supporters.

"*My parents largely inspired my entrepreneurial journey. We moved from China to Australia when I was two, and growing up, I never saw them work a 9 to 5 job. Instead, I witnessed how they were able to start and grow a family business from scratch. Their perseverance over the past two decades was inspirational – it wasn't* an easy life, but it taught me the compounding power of commitment and work ethic."

During high school, Lucy picked up a part-time job and worked as a teacher and taught primary school students. She also helped them prepare for high school entrance exams. It was her first taste of teaching and mentoring, and she had a lot of fun in the role.

"One of the biggest skills I developed during that time, aside from patience when dealing with young kids, is the ability to explain complex topics in a simple way for beginners to understand. I realized it didn't matter how good I was at a subject - if I couldn't effectively explain and communicate it with others."

Another thing that piqued Lucy's interest was cooking. She was amazed to learn from her mother that the same ingredient could be transformed into a completely different dish using a different recipe.

"I find cooking very therapeutic and almost like a creative outlet. I love trying new recipes and perfecting old ones. I also love to cook for others - especially my family."

If you observe cooking as a process, you will initially think it looks like chemistry from many angles – particular ingredients, set processes, and specific ratios. As you explore it further, you may realize it has more to it - confident guesswork, sudden improvisation, boundless experimentation, savvy substitution, handling failure, and

> *I realized it didn't matter how good I was at a subject - if I couldn't effectively explain and communicate it with others.*

crumbling uncertainty in a creative way. A recipe is essential, but a lot depends on the chef. Isn't it?

"*I had always stuck with what I was familiar with and never took the initiative to leave my comfort zone. I wasn't involved in extracurricular activities during my school days and never put my hand up for leadership positions. This left a feeling of emptiness and a little "...what if?" voice in my head. I studied my academic subjects diligently. I was not biased towards any particular subject, but technology always interested me.*"

A brilliant academic record in high school had helped Lucy land a Co-op Scholarship at the University of New South Wales, also known as UNSW, Sydney. The UNSW Co-op Program is a career development scholarship that develops scholars into professionals. The program incorporates industry experience, leadership and professional development, networking, mentoring, and financial support for studies. She elected to pursue her bachelor's degree in Information Systems. As a new chapter of her life started, would she try a new recipe or stick to the traditional one?

"*When the first day of university came along, I promised myself to say yes to every opportunity and to take risks – so that I wouldn't be faced with the same regrets looking back. This fear of regret gradually shifted into a desire to make a tangible impact in communities. I saw university as an opportunity to try new things, and in my first year, I joined six student societies. These societies taught me how to work in a team and think critically. With these experiences under my belt, I co-founded the UNSW Digital Society in my third year. This brought together a mixture of my passion for technology and for sharing these learnings with others."*

There is no single recipe for a successful career, but there are some essential ingredients.

Recipe: A successful career	
Ingredients	**Measurement**
1. Passion	Unlimited
2. Commitment	Inexhaustible
3. Focus	Precise

Time	**Difficulty**	**Serves**
Unknown	Unknown	One person

While studying in the Co-op program, Lucy dabbled in different industries and roles, from technology risk consulting at PwC to being a Head Teacher at Code Camp. These early career opportunities gave her a broader understanding of the technology world and supported her in landing an internship opportunity at AWS.

"I initially came across a LinkedIn post where the hiring manager mentioned they were looking for a part-time intern. I messaged the hiring manager on LinkedIn to express my interest and learn more about the role - that was how the interview process started. I cleared three rounds, and since it was for a non-technical role (Communications & Field Enablement Intern), I was mainly asked questions about my past experiences and any relevant skills I may have for the job."

Lucy started her internship at AWS in May 2020 in the Sales Strategy, Operations & Enablement team. Her work involved building an internal Wiki to provide a centralized repository for Sales teams across ANZ to share knowledge. During this internship, her passion for technology and Cloud Computing grew. She delivered a stellar performance during her internship. Along with outperforming in the internship, she took advantage of all the knowledge and resources within AWS. She achieved 4 AWS certifications during her internship to improve her technical skills. To study for AWS Certifications, Lucy used the following 4-step approach:

Step 1: Scoping – Create a high-level study plan by understanding what you need to study to pass the exam.

"*Before studying for each certification, I put aside 1-2 hours to understand the exam requirements, what resources I should use, and how much time I need to dedicate each week to my cloud learning journey. For example, I first read through the official exam guide when preparing for my Solutions Architect Associate exam. Afterward, I selected the resources I planned to use to prepare for the certifications. Finally, I blocked out 2-4 hours on my calendar each day to study to reach my goal of passing the exam within one month.*"

Step 2: Active listening - Watch video courses and take notes on the key points.

"*I like hand-writing my notes because it helps me remember things better. This step is quite simple: watch a video, write some notes, watch another video, and write more notes. And then, at the end of each study session - review the notes you have written to consolidate your knowledge."

Step 3: Getting Hands-On - Do hands-on labs of the AWS services relevant to the certifications.

"The good thing is, the video courses come with interactive tutorials that help you to navigate through the AWS console and use the services. However, I recommend taking this further and gaining even more experience through AWS workshops. If you head to workshops.aws, you will see over 100 free AWS tutorials. Going through a couple of these workshops will help you become more confident when sitting your exam because you would've had actual hands-on experience."

Step 4: Reinforcing – Do practice questions to reinforce your learnings

"I think, on average, I did around 300-400 practice questions for every AWS certification. That's how many times it took for me to feel ready to sit the exam because there are so many types of questions they can ask, especially in the harder ones like the Solutions Architect Professional exam. My biggest tip is to make sure for questions you don't answer correctly, go back to the video courses to review the content."

When Lucy embarked on studying for cloud certifications, she tried various courses taught by different instructors before coming up with her top recommendations.

"To help you save others time, I recommend the top 5 that worked *for me. Stephane Maarek's Udemy course is concise yet engaging and easy to understand. Adrian Cantrill provides in-depth explanations beyond exam prep, which is useful for real-world AWS projects. Neal Davis balances concision with approachable video courses and practice questions. However, Jon Bonso and Tutorials Dojo had the most valuable AWS practice exams I encountered, with detailed explanations that effectively reinforced the concepts. I also advise leveraging AWS Skill Builder's free study resources straight from the source, which I found very helpful."*

She started with the AWS Certified Cloud Practitioner and achieved all three AWS Associate-level certifications. She followed a logical sequence of completing AWS Certified Solutions Architect Associate first, then AWS Certified Developer Associate, and finally AWS Certified SysOps Administrator Associate. Did she fail any certification exam?

"I failed the AWS SysOps Administrator associate certification twice before passing on the third one. The main reason I failed was that I underestimated the difficulty of the exam and thought I could pass by just studying the theory. However, the exam required a deeper knowledge of AWS that could only be achieved through hands-on experience. However, I also want to point out that it's completely okay to fail AWS certifications once, twice ... or even multiple times! If you learn from your mistakes, don't fear not passing on the first go!"

Through the failures, Lucy learned the importance of applying technical concepts into practice - whether doing hands-on tutorials or building your cloud project. She was religiously following the recipe for a successful career; will she be qualifying for a Micheline star?

"When an opening popped up for an Associate Solutions Architect role, I crossed my fingers and applied. Surprisingly, I was offered the role based on my internship performance. I didn't have to do additional interviews. By getting certified, I probably exhibited the Amazon Leadership principles like Learn and Be Curious and Bias for Action. Transitioning from an AWS Intern to an Associate Solutions Architect at AWS was a straightforward process for me, thankfully. I started fulltime at AWS in Dec 2020."

It was time to add another recipe to her cookbook.

Recipe: Awesome Solutions Architect	
Ingredients	Measurement
1. Technical Knowledge	At par
2. Customer Focus	Obsession level
3. Ownership	100%

Time	Difficulty	Serves
Depends	Hard	Many Customers

"I enjoyed my role to the core. I was helping customers solve business problems, learning rapidly, and connecting and collaborating with colleagues worldwide. I was able to visit new countries for the first time, thanks to AWS. At the same time, I was feeling lost too. I was not very confident in my technical skills at the start. I upskilled through certifications and hands-on projects to bridge the gap. It helped me boost my confidence. I also got help from some amazing mentors in AWS."

By now, Lucy had developed a mindset that everything is learnable. *"I don't know it yet, but I can learn about it,"* got instilled in her attitude. She faced every challenge that came her way as a learning opportunity. It's the attitude that counts most of the time rather than skills. If you ever get caught up in a failed recipe, try turning it around with a twist, approach the problem with fresh eyes, and voila, you get it right. What else was cooking in her kitchen?

"I started my YouTube channel – Tech with Lucy[1], towards the end of my AWS internship. I wanted to provide a way to share my experiences and answer many questions I kept getting asked, like - What tips do you have on passing the AWS Cloud Practitioner Certification? I thought that if I had videos about the questions, I could just send them to others with the same query. I continued to create and share videos on the channel about once a month to help answer common questions that I received from the comments section. I kept engaging and growing the community."

When Lucy started her YouTube journey, she barely knew how to use a proper camera or how to edit videos, and she was quite terrified of uploading videos. She convinced herself just to give it a go because, back in university, she always enjoyed teaching and mentoring others, and YouTube just seemed like the perfect platform for it. The video she published was *"How I passed the AWS Cloud Practitioner Exam in 3 Weeks"*, followed by *"How I passed 3 AWS Exams in 3 Months"*. Were there any viewers for these types of videos?

---

[1]https://www.youtube.com/@TechwithLucy/

"*After making about ten videos, it became pretty clear to me that there was a demand for the type of content I was creating - which, at the time, were videos about my experience working at AWS. I started getting so many comments and messages from viewers who got value out of the content I was sharing - and that gave me the motivation I needed to continue.*"

Lucy's YouTube journey started as a side project to share and document her experiences working in AWS, similar to how she did it for UNSW Digital Society. She uploaded videos regularly while working at AWS. Gradually, Lucy was able to build a following and also begin to monetize the channel. What once started as a method of documenting her journey with the intent of helping others now grew into a full-blown revenue stream. Did it happen overnight?

"*In my first year of creating YouTube videos, I made $0 from it, so I had no idea I could turn it into a full-time career. As with the experience of many YouTubers, I slowly learned how to monetize my channel through ads, sponsorships, and paid products. By the end of the second year of the Solutions Architect job, my YouTube income surpassed the amount I earned at AWS.*"

The growing number of subscribers on her YouTube channel was a testament to the demand for her content. Apart from the financial aspect, seeing the impact she was driving was encouraging. She could not ignore the urge to take the self-employed path. The strong spice of entrepreneurship was probably overpowering all the flavors in her dish. No matter the outcome, she decided to give it a try. It was time to try a new recipe.

"*Now, at that point, I was like, okay, Lucy, if you don't take the risk and try doing YouTube full-time, this might be something you will regret - because you know the channel's growing. You should do what you love, and your videos are helping. My main hesitation was that I enjoyed working at AWS. I had an amazing support network and still miss those days.*"

She decided to take the leap and quit her job in November 2022. Creating content for YouTube was her full-time job. During the early period of self-employment, she was offered a role at Google as a Customer Engineer. She had firmly decided to continue being a freelancer and work towards helping more people and scaling the channel full-time.

Recipe: Successful YouTube Channel	
Ingredients	**Measurement**
1. Market Research	Gap in the market
2. Consistent Approach	High-quality, concise videos
3. Persistent Efforts	Undeterred

Time	Difficulty	Serves
Ongoing	Hard	100K+ Subscribers

"*I focused on beginner-friendly content that reaches a larger audience population and helps people get started on their cloud journey. My content is based on what my viewers want to see instead of just the content I want to create. I keep customer obsession at the top. Sounds familiar?!*"

After leaving her job, Lucy had to adjust her thought process about the work. She had to constantly remind herself that she was no longer an employee with a fixed salary but someone with her own business. She was entirely responsible for the business and her brand. Though it may give you much freedom and flexibility, it can sometimes be scary. You have to be very self-disciplined to stay on track.

"*Even though I don't have a 9 to 5 job now, I still try to stick to 9 to 5 work hours and take regular breaks because if I don't, I will end up overworking or not getting anything done. I'm still trying to figure out the perfect routine and schedule, but in a typical week, I would have blocks of time dedicated to scriptwriting, video recording, and editing. That's 90% of what I need to do to sustain the core YouTube business - but I also spend time working on new business ideas and building my technical skills these days.*"

Lucy admits that success is seldom achieved solo. It requires a strong network of people who believe in you, support you, mentor you, and push you to do your best. She loves the concept of minimalism and believes that less is more. She always tries to remove excess items from her living space and declutters her mind to focus more on things that matter, but she has a different viewpoint regarding networking with people.

> *Being successful requires a strong network of people who believe in you, who support you, mentor you and push you to do your best.*

"*When it comes to networking – More is less. I would say networking is crucial! When people think of networking, many might think it's very scary and intimidating - but it can be amusing. It can help you learn about new job opportunities and gain insights into the industry you typically can't find online. I would recommend taking the initiative to attend industry events, join communities, and reach out to people outside your network to build relationships.*"

She has built up a community of over 100K+ tech & cloud enthusiasts on her YouTube channel. AWS soon spotted her drive to help others through her YouTube channel. She was recognized as an AWS Community Builder[1], which was an endorsement of her contribution to the community.

"*When I first started, I had so much fear around what other people would think, or what if all of this fails - but for me, the potential regret of not giving it a go was much scarier. The key is to find something you enjoy doing and are passionate about. Start small; don't overthink it. Publish that blog. Create that TikTok video. Starting is always the hardest. Build and iterate from there. Once you start building and creating - try not to expect money to come in immediately. Focus on providing value to your target audience, and the rest will come after that.*"

Her YouTube channel is her primary method of contributing back to the community. All of her videos are entirely free to watch. She works with sponsors to make sure the content continues to be free. Has she figured out a long-term plan?

---

[1] https://aws.amazon.com/developer/community/community-builders/

"I used to set 5-year, 10-year plans - but now I'm pleased with where I am in life, from both a career and personal perspective. I have accepted that it's hard to predict the future and set specific goals that I will follow through. Instead, my vision is to continue doing what I'm doing - keep learning, help others, and give back to the community."

With economic uncertainty creeping up in the world, having an additional source of income through a side hustle can provide more financial security and independence. Lucy recommends finding something that lies in the intersection between what you're interested in, what you're good at, and what the world needs.

"For example, if you are interested in personal finance and are the go-to person in your friend circle for money tips, you could start a finance-related YouTube channel. If you enjoy creating tech tutorials and how-to videos, you could start a tech-focused YouTube channel like mine. Just go for it."

Recipe: A fulfilling career	
Ingredients	**Measurement**
1. Your interest	Utmost
2. Your Expertise	Top Notch
3. Customer Demand	High

Time	**Difficulty**	**Serves**
Eventually	Varies	You and your customers

So, what is your recipe for success?

Lucy's AWS journey started when she was 20. During the pandemic, she joined AWS as an intern in May 2020 and became an Associate Solutions Architect after her internship. After two years as an AWS Solutions Architect, she quit her job in Nov 2022 to create videos full-time. The "Tech With Lucy" channel was born out of a desire to help others start a career in the Cloud industry. She is thinking of creating a second channel to share more of the "behind the scenes" of what it's like doing YouTube full-time.

This ex-Amazonian is very grateful to all the mentors, managers, and peers she has had the opportunity to meet and seek guidance from over the years. She is motivated to soak more knowledge to teach it to others through YouTube. Her community following is growing, and aspirants benefit from the content she is creating. She has no plans to stop soon and will keep looking for possible chances to help others - In the end, you only regret the chances you didn't take.

ADVICE

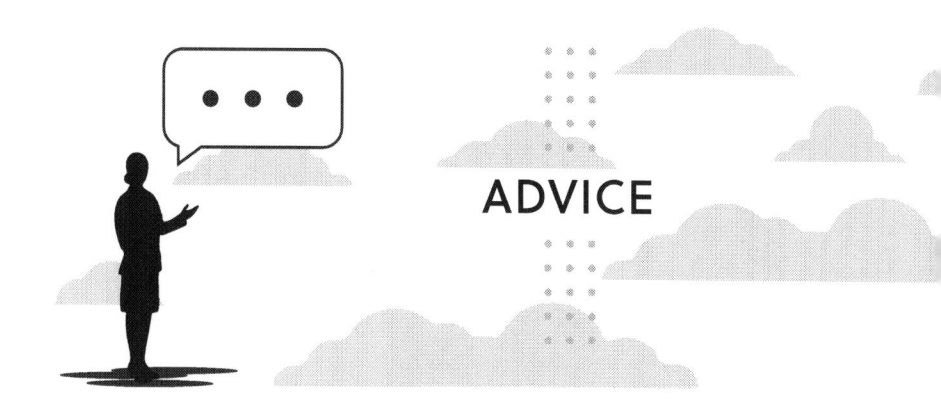

Advice when following a Cloud career path

- **Adopt a growth mindset** - Always focus on growing your knowledge. At any stage, learning should never stop. Talent and ability can be developed through dedication and hard work.

- **Understand the fundamentals** - Make sure you build strong foundations from the start. Basics are vital for success in an endeavor, so invest time and master fundamentals.

- **Stay updated** - Keeping pace with current technological trends and innovations is crucial for a successful career. Remember, a dish tastes the best with fresh ingredients.

ACTION

Actions to take that will drive meaningful progress

- **Build a Portfolio** - Create a GitHub repo or a personal blog where you document all your cloud projects. It's a great way to showcase your skills to potential employers.

- **Start preparing for interviews early** - Interviewing is a skill, and like any other skill, you must learn it. Doing at least one mock interview before the real thing is a good idea.

- **Network, network, network** - Make at least one new meaningful connection every week. Reaching out to people who are either cloud learners or people working in the role you want to be in.

ALERT

Alerts to avoid common pitfalls that can hinder success

- **Not building hands-on skills** - While having a strong understanding of theoretical concepts is essential, it's equally important to have practical, hands-on experience to showcase your skills in an interview and on the job.

- **Not having a clear strategy** - Without a proper plan, getting sidetracked and losing sight of your goals can be easy. A clear strategy will also tell you what not to do.

- **Being impatient** - There is rarely any overnight success. You need to nurture your career through patience and persistence. Give it time while making efforts. Some dishes like career may take time to cook.

The Liberators

Eased the Cloud path for others

Through mentoring, teaching, and community building, they guide newcomers to bridge any gaps. By empowering those around them, they open new routes to the Cloud for all.

The Liberators

The Liberators

Jon Bonso
Co-Founder,
Tutorials Dojo

10   From Deprived Roots,
     To Dojo of Cloud Skills

Neal Davis
Founder,
Digital Cloud Training

11   Got Certified to Start IT Career,
     Now Leading Through Cloud Trainings

Julie Elkins
Senior Exam Prep Curriculum Developer,
AWS

12   Once Leading Scuba Divers,
     Now Guiding Cloud Professionals

From Deprived Roots, To Dojo of Cloud Skills

Jon Bonso
Co-Founder,
Tutorials Dojo

Dojo is a term of Japanese origin that is widely related to the world of martial arts but it has a way wider meaning. It is a place to be humble, learn, practice, teach and commence your journey towards being a better version of yourself.

Do you need to travel solo on this journey?
Shouldn't you help others in their journey as well?

When money is scarce and necessities are precious, you learn its value too early in life. Jon Bonso was born to native Filipino parents in the densely populated and deprived areas of Metro Manila, Philippines. As the second-born child after an older sister, Jon came into a family already stretched thin. His father worked long hours as a low-paid plant mechanic while his mother was a homemaker. In those early years, Jon saw the harsh realities of poverty around him in the neglected neighbourhoods where he lived.

Our family was poor. We used to live in dirty slums and survived on minimal resources. My life in slums maybe actually correlate to the depiction of the early childhood days of the protagonist from the Oscar winning movie Slumdog Millionaire.

At the age of five, a ray of hope shone on Jon's family when his father found work overseas in the Middle East. His father stayed away from the family and worked hard in the scorching temperature of Saudi Arabia to earn livelihood for the family. Though still of modest means, this job allowed Jon, his mother and his sister to move from the overcrowded poverty of Jon's birthplace to a neighborhood with more stability in Metro Manila.

Jon's family had escaped extreme hardship, but financial struggle was still their reality. Early in life, Jon realized that at each stage of his journey, he would face choices that would set his path for years to come. He has to make an informed decision.

> **QUESTION:**
> **How can I help my family?**
> ○ A - I am too young, I can't do anything
> ○ B - Let me pick up some petty jobs to earn extra cash
> **My Answer:** B

Jon began working at a young age, taking on jobs ill-suited for childhood. He hawked newspapers and eggs in the streets and delivered heavy tanks of liquified petroleum gas door-to-door to earn money for his family.

"*After few years, my mother opened a sari-sari store, a small neighborhood shop in the Philippines selling basic goods. I often helped her run it, stocking rice, canned food, and poultry supplies. To bring in extra cash, I would wash jeepneys - the crowded minibuses local to the Philippines that served as public transportation around our area."*

Though just a teenager, Jon bore responsibilities beyond his age. He remained determined to break the cycle of poverty into which he had been born and viewed the world through a unique lens shaped by hardship. He continued his studies through these challenges.

"I was not a stellar student. My grades were pretty average. When I flunked in one of my subjects in college, my parents were there to support me. They never forced me to be a high achiever; rather, they taught me the importance of hard work and consistency even if it did not bring excellent results immediately."

Jon had two dreams in life. The prominent one was joining the military. This dream crossed his mind when he was influenced by the fierceness of soldiers. His other obscure dream was to become a hacker. This one got ingrained when he had watched a movie about hackers and started to wonder what it would be like to be a tech prodigy. This was the starting point of his gravitation towards Information Technology.

QUESTION:

What do I want to be?

○ A - Soldier

○ B - Tech Prodigy

My Answer: B

"I wanted to join the military but I couldn't pursue this profession

because of my short height. But I did get to fulfil my other dream in a much more honest and sophisticated way later in life. And not so surprisingly, I built my whole career in Information Technology."

Academically, Jon considered himself an average student, without the star-pupil status of his older sister (who later became a doctor in the US). But despite his circumstances, Jon successfully completed high school and went on to college to pursue a Bachelor's degree. His family's finance was still sparsely spread, but a consistent flow of income through his father's job and mother's sari-sari store allowed Jon to enrol into college. He studied IT at Mapua University in the Philippines, working diligently to gain the skills for a future in tech.

While doing some part time jobs, Jon graduated with his bachelor's degree in IT by the age of 20. His family had supported him all the way. After graduation, he started applying for jobs immediately, eager to launch into the tech industry without delay.

"In my university days I had developed quite an interest in Cisco networking. Initially, when I had started to look for jobs, I was searching for the role of a Network Engineer. But soon I realized that a Software Engineer earns much more remuneration. So, I started looking for the role of a Software Engineer."

QUESTION:

Which Job profiles should I target?

○ A - Software Engineer

○ B - Network Engineer

My Answer: A

Jon knew the importance of money through the various adversities he and his family had been through. He vividly remembered the time when they almost got evicted from their house as they could not pay the mortgage on time. He was determined to break this cycle of hardship.

Practical and ambitious, Jon pivoted his efforts toward securing a higher-paying Software Engineer position. Jon knew that this role would provide financial stability and career prospects that reflected his skills and drive. He was ready to hit the ground running and prove his worth.

"When I graduated, I got my first job as a Java Programmer at Lawson Software Inc. (now called Infor). I worked diligently there for 2 years and then went to work at HP on similar profile. I also worked briefly at Accenture, and during this period an opportunity came for an overseas job in Singapore."

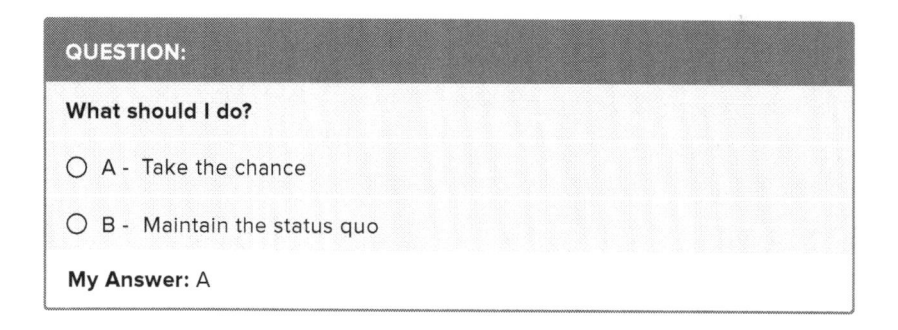

> **QUESTION:**
>
> What should I do?
>
> ○ A - Take the chance
>
> ○ B - Maintain the status quo
>
> My Answer: A

"I left Accenture just 5 months after, to take a chance on a job overseas. One has to take risks and chances in their career for growth and that's what I did. I landed a role as an Application Developer at Crédit Agricole Corporate and Investment Bank, working on a *conditional visa. It was an immense learning experience."*

While in Singapore, Jon received his first exposure to AWS cloud computing. He came across a recruiter from Vancouver hiring tech talent in Singapore for AWS roles in Canada. Intrigued, Jon swiftly created an AWS account to learn more. At his banking job, on-premises servers still dominated, but Jon noticed that cloud technology was the future. As per Jon, the job market is always the most accurate source of truth.

"AWS Cloud piqued my interest. I immediately signed up for it and built my first website project. Unfortunately, I couldn't grasp the opportunity to work for AWS in Canada because it was only limited to Singaporean citizens and I was in the country on a work visa. But gladly through this encounter I came across AWS Cloud Computing which later became the next big thing in IT."

In Singapore, Jon's work visa was tied to the company, and he could not change jobs due to this limitation.

QUESTION:

What can I do to overcome the limitation of work visa?

○ A - Take a chance, look for opportunities with flexible visa

○ B - Maintain the status quo, remain in the same job

My Answer: A

> The job market is always the most accurate source of truth.

At any point when Jon has been faced with a dilemma of taking risks or keep things the way they presently are, he has chosen to challenge the status quo.

After working in Singapore for three years, he started his next job search. This time he cautiously looked for overseas opportunities where visa would not be a limitation. He narrowed in his job search to Australia, where he could apply to become a permanent resident and eventually a naturalized citizen. After securing the required visa he moved to Sydney, Australia. His permanent residency opened plenty of doors for him. Jon was now able to switch between companies within the country more effortlessly.

"*I was a job hopper in my initial years of working in Australia. And with a permanent residency, it was even easier for me to do so. In this process I used to mindfully prepare myself for interviews. I would always try to adapt to the skillset requirement in the job description. If I were not familiar with any framework or services, I would spend my time learning about those things.*"

While working in Australia, Jon began reinventing his professional career. Throughout his career he had primarily worked on backend technologies programming in Java but now he started adding front-end technologies and added JavaScript into his profile. He sensed that the progression in the software world was towards microservices

> *I would always try to adapt to the skillset requirement in the job description. If I were not familiar with any framework or services, I would spend my time learning about those things.*

architectures and Java was not the first choice of language in this advancement. Jon trained himself through various free resources and within a short period of time he became a full stack developer.

"*Your industry will tell you about the right time to reinvent yourself. My time for reinvention had come and I started aiming towards becoming a full stack developer. I began my training with the help of online courses and even paid attention to soft skills like English proficiency. When you are upgrading and upskilling yourself, the job market becomes your north star. You can easily find what is in demand.*"

Having seen the financial struggles in his childhood, Jon wanted to diversify his income streams to improve his finances.

> **QUESTION:**
>
> **How can I build a steady stream of secondary income? (Select all that apply)**
>
> ○ A - Hop on a part-time job
>
> ○ B - Share my knowledge in return for some income
>
> **My Answer:** A and B

Alongside his regular job, he started working on part-time contract positions. Taking on contract work for independent clients provided extra earnings on top of Jon's full-time job. With years of experience to leverage, Jon capitalized on opportunities to generate more revenue.

Though thriving professionally, Jon harboured a latent passion for teaching. When he discovered the Udemy platform, the pieces came together. Jon realized he could share his extensive IT knowledge by creating online courses.

"*I was looking for an opportunity to earn a secondary income. So, I started selling my own Udemy courses. The courses I created were about WordPress tutorials, JavaScript tutorials, Angular and Aurelia framework tutorials etc. It was not a huge income but every avenue of extra income is good. Isn't it?*"

The additional income validated Jon's wisdom in benefiting from his skills while helping others learn. Combining his technical expertise with hidden teaching talents, Jon began publishing video tutorials on Udemy. But how did he come up with the name Tutorials Dojo?

"*I started familiarizing myself with all online learning platforms. I came across Tutorials Point and knew that was the first part of my brand name. It encapsulated my goal of sharing practical skills through instructional materials. For the second half, I chose 'Dojo' - a Japanese word for a training facility.*"

A dōjō is a hall or place for immersive learning, experiential learning or meditation. This is traditionally in the field of martial arts, but has been seen increasingly in other fields. The term literally means "place of the way" in Japanese, where you practice and train the way of anything, as long as the way leads you to enlightenment.

Initially, Jon began blogging under the Tutorials Dojo name with an aim to showcase technical skills for potential future employers;

unbeknownst to him, it would spark something much bigger. What started as a personal platform to exhibit his capabilities slowly evolved into Jon's passion project and full-fledged business. As he ventured into video tutorials, Jon found he could monetize his industry knowledge while helping others learn. Just like aspiring learners dedicate themselves in a dojo, Jon envisioned that his Tutorials Dojo will be a space for people to immerse themselves in technical learning. How do you know you are creating courses on the topics that are relevant to current industry?

True to his mantra that the job market reveals the most accurate truths, Jon let employers' demands guide his course offerings. As he switched between companies in Sydney, Jon had observed AWS cloud services permeating every workplace. First-hand AWS experience at these companies affirmed the undeniable momentum. The abundance of AWS roles signalled skyrocketing adoption. But what does the AWS certification journey of Jon look like?

"*I did not follow a specific structured learning path. I was getting real life experience on AWS in my job. And along with the courses I bought, I was doing lot of hands-on labs on my own in a personal AWS account. It did take me a few attempts to pass some of my certifications but I was able to pass every certification which I had aimed for. I now have around 10 AWS certifications.*"

"*When I was preparing for my first AWS certification - AWS Certified Solutions Architect Associate, I struggled to find good practice tests. There were existing practice tests, but the detailed explanations for each of the questions were missing.*"

> **QUESTION:**
>
> What should I do to address the gap?
>
> ○ A - Take the chance, fill up the missing piece
>
> ○ B - Maintain the Status-quo, wait for someone to create it
>
> **My Answer:** A

Jon's gift of imagination paired up with his spirit of entrepreneurship and he started looking to address the gaps in certification trainings. His breakthrough came in 2018 when he published the first practice test with detailed explanations of answers for AWS Certified Solutions Architect Associate on Udemy, garnering very positive reviews from students. This overwhelming response lit a spark, and Jon knew it was time to scale Tutorials Dojo. Jon and his wife co-founded the company with the name he had first coined for personal blogging. Jon doubled down on creating practice tests for different AWS Certifications. Tutorials Dojo was open to take in more *gakusei, the Japanese word for student.*

When Jon first launched Tutorials Dojo, he continued working as a full-stack developer. However, just a year in, the venture's growth allowed a leap of faith. Jon's income from AWS practice tests and courses eclipsed his corporate salary. Is he going to take the risk? Is he in the state of *youi* (be ready - both mentally and physically)?

"*An individual will face certain risks in their career, even if they work at a full-time job or if they start something of their own, some kind of risk will always be in sight. In my case, I have always had an appetite for a calculated risk. I have a habit of saving and throughout* the years I had saved enough money on which I could live off, if things didn't work out in my favour. But luckily, they did and my risk was worth it."

Though risky, leaving his job to focus on Tutorials Dojo full-time was a deliberate move. When the moment arrived, he took a confident leap, backed by data and driven by ambition. Jon was determined to build something meaningful that matched the effort he had poured in. Going all-in on Tutorials Dojo was the next logical move. He became the *sensei* (sen-say) of Tutorials Dojo, a term reserved for the chief instructor of the dojo.

"Building your own company inevitably brings challenges that require adaptation. For me, a major hurdle was scaling Tutorials Dojo's sales. I realized that providing free, valuable content was crucial for driving sales of Tutorials Dojo's premium offerings. So, I started publishing free cheat sheets covering key AWS services and concepts."

The cheat sheets acted as funnels, allowing learners to sample Jon's expertise at no cost. For those seeking deeper knowledge, the cheat sheets led naturally to Jon's paid practice tests and courses. The free materials served both students and business goals. Learners could access helpful reference resources to reinforce AWS fundamentals across services. Jon leveraged the popularity of the cheat sheets to boost Tutorials Dojo's visibility and trust.

"I knew that relevance would make or break my business. I doubled down on constant market research to spot emerging tech skills in demand by employers."

> **QUESTION:**
>
> **What should I do to keep my courses relevant and updated in the fast-changing world of cloud?**
>
> ○ A - Take the chance, upgrade the courses
>
> ○ B - Maintain the Status-quo, it's too much work
>
> **My Answer: A**

"*I continuously upgraded Tutorials Dojo's offerings based on these insights, branching into creating content for new AWS services and other major cloud service providers. By keeping Tutorials Dojo aligned with real-world needs, we grew into a top destination for AWS and cloud training in just a few years.*"

Jon had been creating video courses on Udemy all along on different technologies. But when his AWS practice tests began selling rapidly, he and his wife decided to halt work on video courses and shift focus solely to practice tests for Tutorials Dojo. At the time, it seemed wise to differentiate from the crowded video course space and play to their unique strength. He needed KIME (kee-may), focus of power.

"*In hindsight, that was a mistake and I wasn't listening to the market correctly. On Udemy's platform especially, comprehensive video courses were selling better and generating more revenue. But I focussed on the practice tests, thinking they would be most useful for students. While still valuable, I realized too late that the market demand signalled video content was king.*"

While painful in the moment, those early missteps ultimately made

Jon a stronger entrepreneur. They refined his vision, imagination and strategy for Tutorials Dojo through the harsh lessons absorbed. Jon emerged committed to continuous improvement however possible. He knew setbacks are part of every founder's journey, but turning them into growth catalysts is the key. He believes in the path of *kaizen*, continuous improvement.

Through his early life hardships, Jon understands clearly that not everyone may be able to purchase his courses. So, he wants to ensure that affordability should not deter someone from pursuing his/her career. He is compassionate about giving back to the community. Along with his paid courses, he has created free blogs, videos, ebooks and more resources to help newcomers master AWS skills. This contribution was recognized by AWS and he was awarded coveted title of AWS Community Builder.

Tutorials Dojo also provides support to the community by answering questions from aspiring cloud enthusiasts on Reddit and other online forums. Jon's contributions as an AWS Community Builder allow him to uplift others while sharing his extensive AWS knowledge. Helping fellow learners also continually inspires and motivates Jon in his own work. After all, a dojo is not just for a single person.

"It is an honor for me to be an AWS Community Builder. It's commendable to see how people from all over the world get to connect with each other for creating awareness about AWS cloud services under one roof."

By making quality Cloud training accessible, he has helped uplift and empower other engineers. Knowing Tutorials Dojo has real, human impact inspires him daily. Though he set out to follow his own path, Jon ended up paving the way for others like him. Seeing the learners thrive, reaffirmed Jon's commitment to keep creating more resources for Cloud learners worldwide.

From humble beginnings in the streets of Manila, Jon carved an unlikely path to the cloud computing mastery. With self-belief and tireless effort, he transformed his passion into a globally recognized cloud training platform, Tutorials Dojo. Though others may call him *shihan* (shee-han), a formal title meaning master instructor or teacher of teachers he prefers to be considered a *sempai* (sem-pai): a senior student who never stops learning!

ADVICE

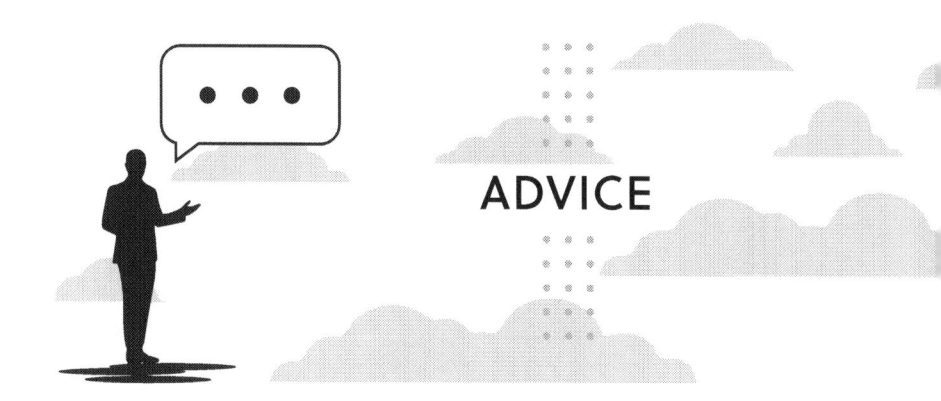

Advice when following a Cloud career path

- **Study the Job Market** - The job market is the ultimate source of truth. You will learn about the industry and the latest booming technologies or cloud services only when you understand the job market thoroughly.

- **Experiment on your own** - Don't be dependent on your employer to provide you with the right training that meets the newest market trend. You have to strive on your own to update yourself with the latest services.

- **Reinvent yourself** - There is always room for improvement. In the IT industry, things change at the drop of a hat. You can only survive those changes of the industry and progress in your career only if you reinvent yourself from time to time.

ACTION

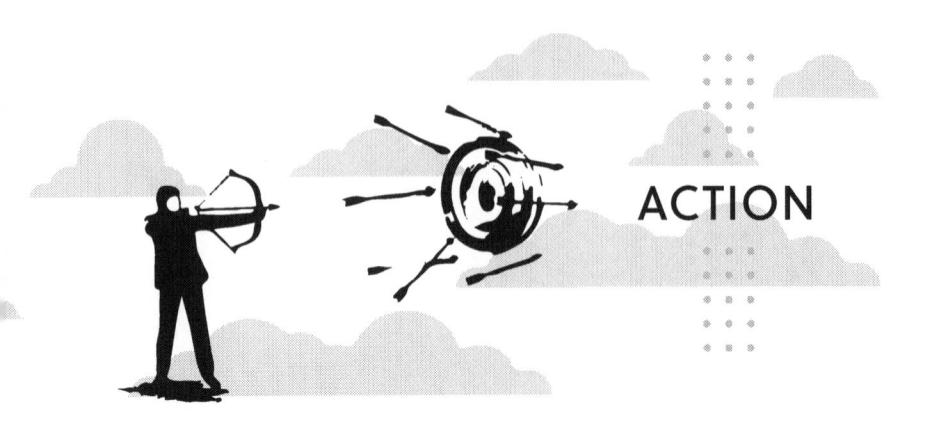

Actions to take that will drive meaningful progress

- **Have Bias for action** - Take actions even when you are not fully assured of the results. Take a chance in learning something new or aiming for something which is outside of your job role just to be benefitted with motive of trying.

- **Develop your soft skills** - Soft skills are as important as your technical skills. You should have the knowledge and the understanding of how to hold a productive conversation with your employers and your clients.

- **Create an appetite for risks** - You can grow in your career rapidly if you took the necessary risks. You don't have to be extremely reckless while taking a risk but some calculated risks can actually take you further in your journey

ALERT

Alerts to avoid common pitfalls that can hinder success

- **Don't be petrified** - In your career, the risks and chances which you want to take will scare you. Certain opportunities are time bound and grasping them can avoid a possible downfall of the future.

- **Don't question your capabilities** - The knowledge that you have is a result of your experiences and it is unique to you. When you question your self based on the merits of other people, you will demotivate yourself. You don't have to compete and compare with anyone else.

- **Don't fail to plan** - You have to plan your journey and your career to a certain extent. The market can change out of the blue and you will only survive it with some beforehand planning.

Got Certified to Start IT Career, Now Leading Through Cloud Trainings

Neal Davis

Founder,
Digital Cloud Training

Unlike most sports, mountaineering lacks widely applied standard rules, strict regulations, and detailed governance, but like other sports, it requires skill, stamina, knowledge, and experience to handle specialized equipment. Reaching a mountain summit is a mind-blowing experience.

Isn't succeeding in life similar to climbing a mountain?

We seek independence and yearn to break free from places where we feel we don't fit in. We desire to make our own choices and shape our futures with the inexperience of youth. This was true for Neal Davis, who had felt that he would never be able to fit into the traditional school system. When he got the chance, he decided to drop out of school. As in most cases, circumstances dictate the path forward, and our actions drive it further.

Born in Cardiff, Wales, to English parents, Neal was the middle child in a family of two older sisters and one younger brother. Neal's parents were diligent professionals - his father was in a banking job while his mother administered youth centers. At age six, Neal's family returned to England, settling into the pleasant neighborhood of Beaconsfield in Buckinghamshire County, which became their new home. As Neal grew up, he had the opportunity to study in one of the best schools in the area. But did he enjoy school?

"I did not have a good experience at school. I was a mischievous student and never enjoyed the way education was imparted. My motivation to educate myself through traditional school gradually depleted over the years. So, I thought quitting school would be the right thing to do. After taking this step, I was unsure what to do, but I had the urge to be in the world on my own and do things the way I wanted."

Neal was determined to drop out of school at 16, foregoing further academics. He disliked the teaching style and struggled to get along with his teachers. With his naive reasoning, he decided to quit formal education.

"I think my parents realized I would always be very self-driven and determined to follow a distinct path. They tried dissuading me but soon accepted that I would drop out. Understandably, they weren't entirely happy that I passed up the educational opportunities many others would be grateful for. In hindsight, I should have appreciated those chances more. We all make mistakes in life. The important thing is that we learn from them and move forward."

After abruptly ending his schooling, Neal immediately entered the workforce to start earning money on his own. His income potential was limited as a 16-year-old with no experience or qualifications. He started taking on part-time jobs and lower-wage work. In the early days, his parents supported him when he struggled to make a living.

"*In mountain climbing, you are not facing an opposing team like in other sports. Mountain climbers are pitted against both the unpredictable forces of nature and their limitations. The same is true in life, too. With no experience and qualifications, I was battling to find a steady job.*"

After a few years, the free and independent lifestyle Neal had once been excited about lost its luster. To get by, he worked factory jobs, worked as an electrician, and even worked as a chef. Even though they were tough jobs to do and for long hours, none of these odd jobs provided stable income in the long term. There was a period when Neal experienced what it was like to be broke, with no security.

"*Once I was on my own, I quickly realized the limited opportunities I had. Quitting school was likely the wrong decision, looking back. At the time, I had such a strong need for independence, to find my way and control my destiny and earning potential. I had gathered some experience working in odd jobs and knew I had no good prospects for my future. The pain of not having a secure future gave me enough focus and energy to take action and figure something out for myself before it was too late.*"

When Neal lost sight of the peak during his climb, he reconnected with an old high school friend who shared how he had advanced his career by getting IT certifications. With technology booming in the 1990s, Neal learned of others finding success and stability in the industry through certifications alone. Could IT be the technique Neal was searching for to climb the cliff of his career?

> *I had never considered that you could self-study for a career not requiring a degree. Especially looking back 20-25 years, most high-paying trades mandated college degrees, and even blue-collar jobs expected formal training. The idea that I could just pick up books, learn in my own time in the luxury of my house, take some exams, and get into a potentially lucrative field – was an eye-opener. I was surprised to learn that many people started working based on certifications and not necessarily through a degree from an accredited university. Many assured me I could do the same and start my journey without formal education. I knew I had to try it too !*

Neal changed his approach for the climb but never lost sight of the peak. He borrowed study materials from his friend and pursued the CompTIA A+ certification, which served as his base camp. After succeeding in his first credential, Neal wasted no time going for more - including the Microsoft Certified Systems Engineer and Cisco certifications. He had finally found a promising terrain and started building the stamina for the IT job market. But were these certifications enough for him to enter the IT workforce?

"It wasn't an instant success story - get certified and automatically get a job. That wasn't the reality then; it's not a reality now and won't be a reality in the future. You need more than just certifications. It took a while and several exams before I got my first help desk role of resetting passwords and basic troubleshooting."

While studying, Neal was working at a company in Birmingham processing paperwork for benefits applications. Through that role, he was able to move into IT support as he gained certifications. The company noticed he had valuable skills beyond his initial hiring purpose.

"You have to start somewhere, so that's what I did. I never stopped learning and taking certification exams, even after getting that first job. I just kept learning throughout my whole career. The IT field is vast, with constant new developments. The right certifications open doors, but real success comes from always striving to expand knowledge and skills."

After several months, Neal left that job for a role at AT&T, which

> It wasn't an instant success story - get certified and automatically get a job. That wasn't the reality then; it's not a reality now and won't be a reality in the future.

he considers his first proper IT position. The AT&T role was also a help desk position, but Neal progressed from first to second to third-line support. He provided IT support for various car manufacturing plants across the UK. A few years later, after gaining experience at multiple companies, Neal landed a job at Teksys, an IT firm where he worked for about four years. He was introduced to consulting and providing technology services to educational institutions and corporations there. By the end of his tenure, Neal was working as a subcontractor for Microsoft in Reading, UK, through Teksys. Was the peak in sight?

"*I had gained enough experience and was looking for a new endeavor. Having lived and worked most of my life in the UK, I thought of moving to a new country. A few friends who had relocated to Australia shared their positive experience of the appealing work culture and lifestyle there. I had a solid IT background and credentials, so I decided to leap and apply for permanent Australian residency. My application was quickly accepted, and I moved to Australia in 2008 as a permanent resident.*"

Upon moving to Australia, Neal's first employer was UXC Connect, where he worked for more than three years as a Solutions Architect. This included pre-sales consulting, architecting solutions, and project delivery. He then switched to HP in a similar role, where he got to work on more complex large-scale projects. While he was building his career in IT, did Neal have time to nurture his passion for mountaineering?

"*After nearly 15 years building my tech career, I decided it was time for a sabbatical and to pursue my other passion formally. Three *years into working at HP, I quit my job to climb some of the highest peaks, spending most days in the Himalayas and Andes. I also did adventurous rock climbing in spots like Yosemite and Indian Creek.*"

At the height of his career, Neal carved out a year and a half just for traveling and mountaineering. It's rare for people to step away when things are going well, but Neal recognized he needed time to refuel. He wanted to reconnect with parts of himself beyond just career ambition.

The mountains had constantly renewed Neal's spirit and served as a valuable reset. To pursue this passion without distraction required pressing a pause on work. Those months of climbing, trekking, and reflecting had proved therapeutic for him. He had accomplished a dream by summiting those epic peaks. Deliberately making time for yourself demonstrates what you value most. He was grateful that he had the courage to temporarily trade keyboards for cliffs, a decision that enriched every aspect of his life.

Upon returning from his extended sabbatical, Neal did not immediately rejoin the workforce. Instead, he noticed cloud computing rapidly gaining momentum as an emerging focal point in technology. Though he had limited hands-on cloud experience up to that point, he foresaw soaring demand for cloud engineers.

"*This was around 2016, and the cloud rapidly emerged as a hot new technology. I spent about two and a half months fully dedicated to Cloud certifications - earning the three AWS Associate level certifications and two Azure certifications through intensive studying. I used courses from A Cloud Guru, Udemy, and Pluralsight* to study. With over 15 years of experience, I wasn't worried about needing a degree for credibility at that point in my career. I like to use certifications as a differentiator to stay ahead of the curve."

With his extensive experience, Neal could have obtained a new job right after returning from his sabbatical. Then why take a few months' break to study and get certified?

"IT certifications helped me start my career, and I continued using them to progress. I've seen it repeatedly - folks I worked with who didn't keep learning fell behind on opportunities and feared redundancy. I simply kept myself equipped with proficiencies in areas that are in high demand. So I kept moving up, never worrying about job security. I never got laid off, but I was confident I would get a new job immediately if it ever happened. Continuously learning gives me the edge and resilience."

After earning his cloud certifications, Neal soon found a job at NTT Communications. This first mainstream cloud role involved building hybrid solutions and custom private clouds, giving him tremendous hands-on experience in one year. Neal was then presented with an opportunity to rejoin HP as an Enterprise Architect.

Neal had already spent nearly two decades building an accomplished IT career. At this senior level, he was expected to focus on high-level management and strategy. However, his passion

> *I like to use certifications as a differentiator to stay ahead of the curve. I simply kept myself equipped with proficiencies in areas that are in high demand.*

remained hands-on work and executing innovative projects. It was a completely different terrain. This misalignment with expectations presented a conflict but also an opportunity. He had always been independent, ever since leaving school at 16. Now, he saw a chance to do something himself and make a change.

"*I was looking for opportunities, and I think when you have your mind in the right place and you're looking for something, the opportunities start popping up. I investigated a few options of what I could do, and building an education company was one of them. The first thing I did to get started was to create practice tests. That was because I had been studying and using various practice tests. On some platforms like Udemy, I saw that people were making a lot of sales with practice tests, and I thought it was amazing! I enjoyed writing and liked the documentation work, so I thought, why not give that a go and see if I can make some money doing that online.*"

"*At the time, I didn't know how it would shape. I had been thinking about various business ideas - consulting and toying with different things. As you go through ideas entrepreneurially, you realize the challenges and reasons that something may not work how you want it to. Also, how does one find customers? Most of the time, some of these ideas don't work out either. Nevertheless, creating practice test content seemed straightforward. I could put in the time to create good content and put it out there to see what happens. So, I started creating practice tests while working at my job, just in my spare time. It started working quite well, so I thought, okay, this makes sense. Selling things digitally online has a lot of advantages - infinite scalability, low costs to start, and marketplaces like Udemy find customers for you.*"

Although there are obvious risks in mountain climbing, you can mitigate most of the risks with experience, solid training, reliable equipment, physical fitness, teamwork, and sound judgment. It was a risk leaving the stable job, but he was ready to take a calculated risk. His practice tests were making a bit of money, though not enough to replace his consulting salary. He didn't have a detailed plan with specific goals but wanted to try it. He knew he wanted to focus on growing the education business and see where it could go. Neal's wife, Christiane Wolf, joined him full-time, and together, they focused entirely on growing their online education company – Digital Cloud Training (DCT).

"When starting the business in 2018, we published practice tests for the AWS Certified Solutions Architect Associate and AWS Certified Cloud Practitioner certifications. Those are the most popular certifications, probably accounting for 90% of the AWS certification activity. We expanded into video courses covering the same certifications once those practice test products performed well."

Between Neal and his wife, she handles marketing and promotion while he focuses on creating courses and scaling the business. They have seen rapid growth and progress in a short period, but there is still much more potential to realize. A significant challenge education providers like them face is building the right team. Finding course creators that work to their standards can be difficult, as developing courses is time-intensive.

"From a marketing standpoint, we've always had a presence on Udemy and our website. Udemy has been fantastic for us. As Udemy is a large marketplace with extensive reach, it exposes countless people to our brand, many of whom purchase additional offerings directly from us. So Udemy is a sales platform and a funnel driving new business."

"As we've achieved rapid growth, sustaining that momentum means expanding our catalog. So, we have built a growing team of staff and instructors and are bringing many new courses out. We also expanded into live training boot camps that can help learners build real-world cloud skills and find employment."

Neal has been contributing actively to the AWS community as well. He is currently an AWS Community Builder[1] and has been for a couple of years for putting out a lot of free content for learners. Neal sees it as an excellent opportunity to contribute, especially as

---

[1]https://aws.amazon.com/developer/community/community-builders/

he has witnessed the dramatic growth of the community over time. When Neal pops into the Community Builder Slack channel now, he sees so many participants - evidence of how much it has expanded. Contributing to the community has also helped his business, and he gets to hear the success stories of people who have benefited from his courses.

* * *

Neal's journey illustrates the power of perseverance, adaptability, and maintaining one's sense of purpose. He began working at age 16 after dropping out of school, struggling to find direction and stability in those early years. He gained skills in the booming IT industry through self-study and certifications, creating his career path outside traditional education. His relentless drive to keep learning and stay relevant enabled him to thrive in technology's ever-changing landscape for decades.

What he loves about the IT and cloud industry is hearing people's stories of their career journey, which often mirror his own. He went from an uncertain future to building a fantastic career and helping others discover opportunities to transform their lives and careers just as he did.

Advice when following a Cloud career path

- **Pursue it with patience** - It will take some time to find what works best for you, and then it will take more time to improve. It won't be easy; it could get complicated, but it will be worth your efforts.

- **Upgrade yourself** - In the IT industry, the ones who have developed their knowledge to a higher level are less likely to get overlooked by employers. Upgrade your knowledge, improve your skillset, and gain more experience.

- **Build a good profile** - Currently, your resume details aren't the only information that is considered. Your presence in the community, attendance at important events, and online interactions are all mustered up when the decision to hire you is made.

ACTION

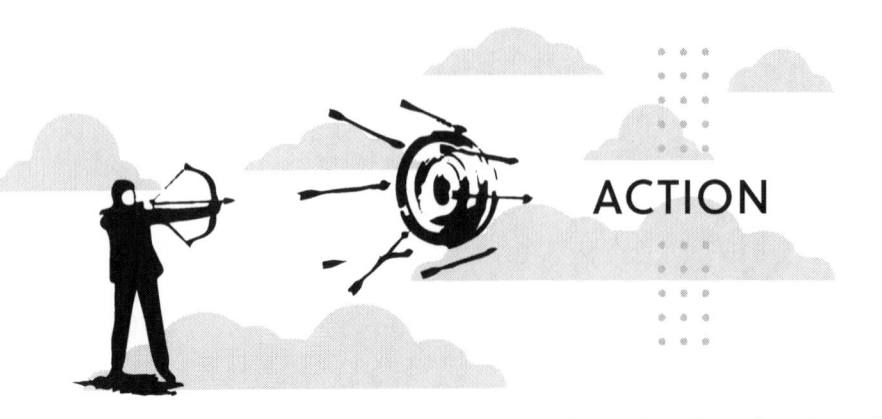

Actions to take that will drive meaningful progress

- **Go for certifications** - At least have one certification, or aim for one when you are just starting. If you do it right, certifications will be the first stepping stone in your journey.

- **Be ready to learn** - Always be willing to learn something new and relearn something you already know. There are plenty of updates taking place every often. And to stay current, you need to learn what you don't know.

- **Look for better job opportunities** - You need to work in spaces where you can get adequate hands-on experience. Even if it appears to be in the role of a junior, just do it. You will surely make progress with doing more practical work.

Alerts to avoid common pitfalls that can hinder success

- **Not going deep enough** - You must explore every aspect of your profession. You have to get some certifications, but you also need hands-on experience. If you only focus on one aspect, you will lack in another area.

- **Not focusing on your domain** - Focus on your professional background, whether in IT or any other field. Concentrate on the domain you have experience in unless you want to change that.

- **Not networking enough** - It is essential to network within the community/workspace. You can quickly get recommendations, references, and new work opportunities if you have built a strong network.

Once Leading Scuba Divers, Now Guiding Cloud Professionals

Julie Elkins
Senior Exam Prep Curriculum Developer,
AWS

To attempt a successful, safe and enjoyable scuba dive into the ocean's depths, you will need to gain the physical strength, necessary knowledge, and specialized training.

What if the mighty ocean gets replaced by the ever evolving Cloud technology?
Will your skills still be relevant for Cloud career journey?

Have you thought of growing up on a beach and exploring a magnificent coral reef in your full Scuba diving gear every week? Sounds like a daydream, right? This dream was the everyday reality of Julie Elkins who grew up on the Surfside Beach, a small town just south of Myrtle Beach City in South Carolina, U.S. Julie's routine involved frequent visits to the waterfronts of Mrytle beach helping her family's scuba diving business, along with her parents and her younger brother.

The shimmering seaside was more than just scenery or picturesque backdrop for Julie, it was her family's livelihood. Julie's father lived by these words "in a family business, the business comes first". Every family member played their part in the success of the dive shop.

"*I loved working at the dive shop. It meant a lot of time out on the boat and in the open water. We sold diving equipment and we also trained people in scuba diving. We taught Open Water, Advanced Open Water, Dive Master, and other speciality certifications to the scuba diving students. As I helped them learn new skills during their training, I realized I loved teaching and helping others.*"

These early experiences created an opening for a room which she would later enter in her life. There goes a saying that, the sea imprints its mark on those raised near the shore. For Julie, the ocean was a lifelong friend - its mysteries and creatures capturing her imagination. Of all its inhabitants, she most adored the sharks and the manatees. Their grace and power reminded her of Ocean Ramsay, the inspiring and audacious female free diver advocating for marine life. However, Julie's greatest inspiration dwelled much closer to home. Her major role model in life has always been her father.

At the time when Julie was working at the dive shop there were hardly any female divers. The decks were dominated by weathered men - all the boat captains, instructors and dive masters were males. Buoyancy devices (A lifejacket, also known as a Personal Flotation Device (PFD)) came sized for their broad shoulders, not the slender frames of aspiring women. This was a timid obstruction for undaunted Julie. Two summers she devoted to mastering her craft and practiced to become a dive master. But her dream was shattered when she couldn't get her diving instructor's license because of her Type 1 diabetic condition. Nevertheless, she proudly watched her younger brother become the youngest certified master captain of their time.

The dive shop was a major part of Julie's life. She had to manage the shop and school simultaneously. Despite of a busy schedule outside of school, Julie remained a brilliant student throughout her school life and graduated high school with honours. She was a perfect juggler.

"*I attended school and also worked at our shop after school hours. My dad always taught me to be disciplined while managing multiple things in life. I would always organize my tasks, create calendar notes and schedule everything beforehand. This habit of organizing and time management helped me even in college when my life became far more hectic but I never missed a single deadline.*"

Sometimes divers use a diving line for easy navigation - wish these lines were drawn for career too! In college, Julie was unsure about her career path. She was studying to get her degrees in both teaching and marine biology. Julie was more interested in teaching, but she also took marine biology classes as it would benefit their family business. Her passions pulled her in two directions, unable to chart a single course.

When Julie was in her final year of college, her father relocated their dive shop from the bottom of the highway 501 bridge to a sports mall. While working at the new location, Julie met a woman from a law firm who was looking to hire a paralegal. After her insistence Julie agreed and traded her wetsuit for a pressed blazer.

With degrees relating to teaching and marine biology but choosing to start her career in law, it seemed like an unexpected detour. She wondered if she was perplexed about what she wanted to do after college. But sometimes it is ok to be confused. Isn't it?

"*I started working as a paralegal right after college. Soon, I developed an interest in researching and understanding law and all the legal terms associated with it. I enjoyed working as a paralegal for as long as I remained at that position.*"

A big change happened when Julie was 24 - her dad sold their family dive shop and moved to Barbados for retirement. Up until then, she had been working part-time at the dive shop while pursuing her career as a paralegal and working at the law firm. That marked *the end of an era.*

"*I was overwhelmed and heartbroken because our shop was an integral part of my life. I had dreams of raising my children someday in the same environment that I grew up in. But now that dream will never see the light of the day.*"

Over time, the dive shop became a fond memory as Julie started a new chapter in her life. She got married and she and her husband moved to Virginia. Soon, they became parents and Julie happily focused on embracing her motherhood. She left full-time work to be a stay-at-home mom. When the kids started school, Julie took a part-time job at her husband's financial firm to have a small role outside the home. Her attention was still focused mainly on family life.

After a 12-year hiatus from full time work to raise her children, Julie resumed her professional career in 2010. She began working for a financial planning company. This new finance job, posed many challenges for Julie. Coming from a background in law, she had to learn a lot in the financial sector. She was in uncharted water. A dive from law books to the books of finance was deep indeed. Had she enough oxygen in her diving tank?

"*I started working for this company without any prior analysis or preparations for the job. The company paid for the training and certifications of their employees but I was not good with numbers and every learning opportunity was a steep curve for me. That marked a low point in my career and so I started looking for a new job.*"

In search of better work opportunities, Julie came across an opening with the National Science Foundation (NSF) for a government contractor role. She applied and secured the job, starting as an administrative assistant in July 2014. She was determined to learn all she could in this position and see where it might lead. Julie remained open to new possibilities trusting the currents of change to guide her journey.

"*The contract that I worked on managed the IT infrastructure* for the National Science Foundation. We had to manage their data centre and the infrastructure. I realised it had been a while since I had worked primarily with computers. My colleagues comprised of senior Windows Engineers, Security Specialists, Linux Engineers and Database Administrators. I was amazed at how much they all knew about IT and how much I did not. I wanted to learn that and all of it, too."

Julie had a craving for learning new things to advance her career. She never wanted to be a small planet stuck in a blackhole. She started to assist the IT professionals by helping them with bits and pieces of their work. One of the engineers at work soon started trusting Julie for tasks related to SharePoint.

Eager to become fluent in the IT jargons and technologies, Julie started taking SharePoint courses. She wanted to gain the expertise to excel at the work being handed to her. It was not just a checkbox activity for her. Slowly but meticulously, Julie was building up her IT knowledge. She approached each new task as an opportunity to upgrade her skills.

"I was struggling to understand SharePoint initially and relied on a mentor for helping me in my learning. I tried to set up my own lab environment and after crashing it for the third time, I had to acknowledge the fact that I was missing the basic IT fundamentals. This was a reality check and it hurt. So, I took a step back and started with CompTIA A+ certification. It took me three attempts to successfully pass it. And then I did Microsoft Windows administrative fundamentals certification. Though difficult, those early certifications were like my baby steps into the IT field."

Julie took the time to fill in gaps in her understanding instead of giving up. Building a strong foundation, allowed her to better grasp more advanced technologies that she was going to dwell into. She had her own uncommon standards to live up to. During the fourth year of her employment, NSF had started migrating their infrastructure and applications to the Cloud and they chose AWS as a Cloud service provider.

"*I noticed that all the Project Managers and Program Managers were strictly instructed to learn AWS, if they wanted to work on the contract there after. As an administrative assistant, this rule didn't officially apply to me. But I was determined to learn and progress like my professional co-workers. Even though it wasn't required for my role, I set a goal to earn all the AWS certifications I could.*"

In the second half of 2018, Julie began preparing for AWS certifications. However, she soon realized she lacked few more necessary fundamentals to navigate through the Cloud successfully and needed a different type of equipment for this dive. Without a solid grasp of core concepts, advanced AWS felt like diving into the deep ocean without an oxygen tank. Self-doubt and questions threatened to pull Julie under the current. Seeking a lifeline, she bought a Linux Academy course on Udemy. The visual interactive diagrams in the course shone light on the Cloud foundations like a beacon in the darkness. This lighthouse guided Julie to safer shores.

> 💡 Julie took the time to fill in gaps in her understanding instead of giving up.

With each new day, her IT basics grew stronger, like skills honed through repetition. By late 2018, Julie felt ready to plunge into swirling AWS currents with confidence. Her Cloud journey had truly just begun. There was no stopping her now.

"Everything I learned from the Linux Academy course was helpful in connecting the dots and filling in the needed fundamentals when I did AWS Certified Solutions Architect Associate certification and the AWS Certified Developers Associate Certification. I was determined to conquer it all and hence went for it one after the other."

"My next milestone, AWS Certified Sysops Administrator Associate certification turned out to be a real struggle. AWS was still pretty new for me and I did not have a proper hands-on experience either. So, I would google sysops questions and then answered them with my understanding and knowledge. And that helped me get through it."

Like ascending a mountain, Julie used certifications as stepping stones to build her IT knowledge. Each new credential became a foothold pushing her higher up the Cloud peak. She didn't let the desire for comfort rule her. The associate certifications formed the base camp for Julie's AWS journey. It grounded her learning with core concepts before tackling advanced heights. From this firm foundation, AWS professional certifications now came into view at the distant summit.

> 💡 *Each new credential became a foothold pushing her higher up the Cloud peak. She didn't let the desire for comfort rule her.*

"When I went for the AWS Certified Solutions Architect Professional certification, everyone on my team at the NSF laughed at me because everyone thought that I wouldn't pass it. So, I overprepared for it and nailed that certification too."

By incrementally working through certifications, Julie was able to steadily strengthen her abilities and understanding over time. Each new certification marked an achievement that motivated her to keep advancing. Around that time, Julie saw an open job position posted on LinkedIn for an AWS Training Architect at Linux Academy. In March 2019, Julie left the NSF contract and joined Linux Academy to further expand her skills. The founder, Anthony James, impressed Julie with his tireless enthusiasm for helping others learn. Adrian Cantrill also became an invaluable mentor, generously sharing his deep AWS knowledge.

Julie also appreciated Linux Academy's employee training opportunities. She spent extra hours absorbing everything she could. The supportive environment facilitated rapid growth. There she also discovered online Slack communities and becoming a member was one of the best career decisions she made.

"Something that extremely helped me and solved a lot of my queries was the slack communities at Linux Academy. Joining a community like slack or discord gives beginners an access to engage in discussions that eventually aids into better understanding of difficult concepts. Some Slack communities also have a home lab channel where they share projects and learners can replicate that and build their own projects."

"With every certification that I was completing, I was investing my time and energy into building projects. Free projects are available online for learners. AWS has range of free build projects that anyone can work on to gain experience. One such project that I built from scratch was a WordPress site."

While Julie knew hands-on Cloud experience was crucial too, she also valued certifications for structuring her learning journey. She has found her diving line, and she clung on to it, while propelling her career. After the AWS Certified Solutions Architect Professional certification, Julie also completed the AWS Certified DevOps Engineer Professional certification. And with both the AWS professional level certifications completed, Julie now aimed for the specialty certifications. Onward and upward.

The path grew steeper but each accomplishment fuelled her momentum. The journey itself was the reward. She straightaway started with one of the hardest specialty certifications which was not something most Cloud engineers would do.

"I started my specialty certifications with the most difficult one, the AWS Certified Advanced Networking. I realised it was a big mistake but I had already jumped into it. And at Linux Academy there was a course for Advanced Networking Specialty so I took that and it helped me get certified."

At this point, Linux Academy had merged with A Cloud Guru. And all the operations were then being conducted in the name of A Cloud Guru which later got acquired by Pluralsight.

"At A Cloud Guru, my co-worker, Kesha Williams, and I were building a recommendation engine which would suggest corresponding A Cloud Guru courses to learners. Since we were already working on machine learning and since I was learning so much from Kesha, I thought this was the right time to go for the AWS Certified Machine Learning Specialty certification."

"There was also a course developed by another colleague, Mike Chambers, for the AWS Certified Machine Learning – Specialty exam at the Linux Academy which turned out to be extremely crucial in preparing for this certification."

Along with her AWS certification streaks, Julie also loved interacting with the AWS community. Like a thriving coral reef, the AWS community teemed with life and knowledge. Julie cherished diving in this vast spread ocean, both learning from and giving back to fellow Cloud explorers. Their collective insights enriched her own understanding far beyond what any textbook could provide. So, when Julie heard of the AWS Community Builder[1] program, she dove right in - to apply.

---

[1]https://aws.amazon.com/developer/community/community-builders/

"*It was one of the best moments for me when I got accepted into the program. In the program, there are events being hosted for all the community builders, free access to trainings from Cloud Academy, discount on the re:Invent ticket and a lot of other support system available for the members. Also, there is a dev.to community for AWS builders[1] where members post incredible articles.*"

After honing her skills through certifications, experience, and community, Julie was ready to explore a role inside AWS. But landing a role at AWS proved a voyage with obstacles, probably a bigger one than all of above. Her first attempt, was to apply for Technical Curriculum Architect. But, Julie's experience fell short of this distant horizon. Next, she applied for Technical Lab Developer, yet again, her coding skills was not seaworthy enough yet for those rough water.

Finally, in her third attempt she got successful when she got referred by her mentor and former colleague, Mark Richman, for the role of a Technical Curriculum Developer - a position that aligned with her strengths. Julie has picture perfect memory of her interviews at AWS. Her mentor's reference was a tailwind, speeding Julie's sails. During the preparation for the interview, he helped her navigate tricky tides. His wisdom and encouragement buoyed Julie across the finish line.

"*The first interview was a technical round. My process to prepare myself for this interview was similar to my SysOps certification. I

I prepared answers for those questions and went back and forth to see how well I could answer.

---

[1] https://dev.to/aws-builders

searched google for AWS technical interview questions and other general technical questions and noted them all. Then I prepared those questions and went back and forth to see how well I could answer. I probably over prepared for that, but it helped."

"My second interview round was the loop interview. For this interview, initially during my preparation, I was only paying attention to my presentation. But my mentor guided me to focus on Amazon Leadership Principles[1] and not just the presentation. I started researching for that and quickly realised that AWS is serious about them. So, I wrote about my experiences exhibiting leadership principles in the star format right from when I was in the NSF and up till A Cloud Guru."

"I spent around 60 hours in preparations for the technical and loop interview altogether. And out of that, I spent almost more than 30 hours just for the leadership principles. And then 30 hours preparing for my projects and presentations. You can't prepare for all questions, but if you prepare well, you will likely only have to deal with one or two unknown questions rather than ten."

During her AWS loop interview, Julie was worried that she had veered off course when asked about the content reviews process. Up until now she was creating and reviewing the content she created

> You can't prepare for all questions, but if you prepare well, you will likely only have to deal with one or two unknown questions rather than ten.

---

[1] https://www.amazon.jobs/en/principles

herself, whereas AWS content development has a well-defined and through review process. But this didn't deter her candidacy, soon an offer came her way.

By then, Julie had earned most of the existing AWS certifications through diligent study. Now on the AWS training team, she deliberately pursued the remaining certs. After completing all available AWS credentials, Julie received the prestigious golden jacket as recognition - a trophy for remarkable tenacity.

"Throughout all my certification exams preparation I would always try to find focused training where the fundamentals of that certification were taught in depth. And for every certification training course I took, I also had a project that I built to ensure I was learning and getting that hands-on experience. I would also refer the exam guide, solve a lot of practice questions, and visit sites like Reddit and LinkedIn to learn about exam experiences that were shared by others. Another key factor that really helped me was a good mentor. I have acquired a few mentors along my path. But I still have my original mentor from the National Science Foundation, and still I talk with him daily."

The golden jacket symbolizes the relentless hard work, firm determination and unshaking resilience of Julie's Cloud journey. But she remains focused on the path forward, not past achievements. With an explorer's curiosity and passion for knowledge, Julie's exciting

> 💡 Another key factor that really helped me was a good mentor. I have acquired a few mentors along my path.

voyage is only beginning. She has become a perpetual learner.

In addition to her role at AWS, Julie remains actively involved in the Cloud community. She has built a robust following on LinkedIn, where she regularly shares knowledge and helps others pursue IT skills development and certifications. She enjoys giving back by supporting newcomers looking to gain Cloud expertise and progress professionally. For Julie, community engagement provides fulfilment beyond her day job. She finds purpose in uplifting others on their skilling journey just as her mentors helped her. By dedicating time to public learning, Julie hopes to widen the circle of Cloud mastery.

"When I was just starting my Cloud journey, I did not know where to find AWS training. I bought my first training course for the AWS Certified Solutions Architect – Associate certification from Udemy. I later found Linux Academy (before I was hired as an employee), but could not afford that monthly subscription cost. One of the reasons I'm so active in the community is because learning and training should be available for anyone. At AWS, we want to "meet the learners where they are" and then help them to upskill further. So, daily in my job and personally out in the community, I try my best to help people's journey into AWS better."

Julie's inspirational path shows that goals once unimaginable, may just be waiting within reach, unlocked by optimism, drive, and belief in our own potential. When starting her Cloud journey, Julie lacked guidance on training options. Just as patient mentors illuminated Julie's way, she now strives to meet learners where they are and empower their growth.

By actively sharing her knowledge, Julie hopes to lift others up on their up-skilling journey as well. Her story proves that progress relies not just on our own efforts, but on creating a rising tide that lifts all ships. Julie's compassion and wisdom will continue rippling outwards for years to come.

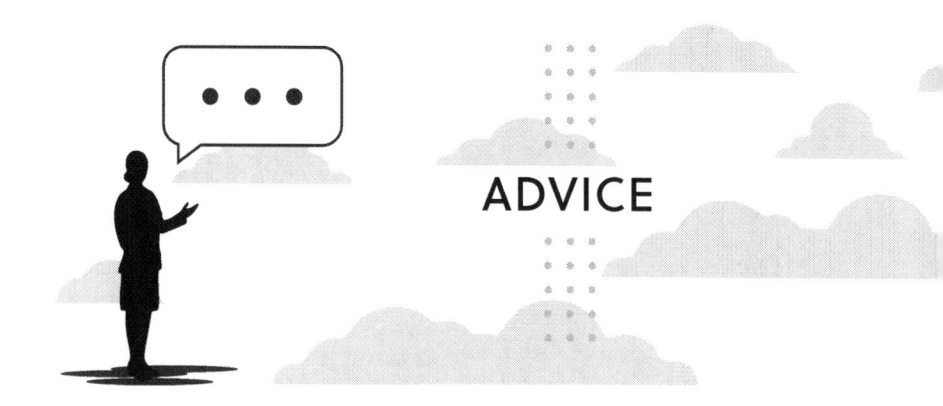

Advice when following a Cloud career path

- **Know where to dive** - Research to find - What job? Which role? Which domain? What skill gaps do I have? Clearly identify the direction you are going to explore, stay focused and build your skills.

- **Be a stickler** - Once you set your goal, chalk your learning path, set your schedule, check progress, apply course correction, but treat it as a deadline, and don't miss it. Check it off and move on.

- **Personalize your learning** - Not everyone learns the same way. Find out what works well for you, is it a video training, or a book or a hands-on exercise? Should I learn every day? Or every other day? Early in the morning? Or just before my bedtime? Should I join some prep-groups? Know what is the most effective method which suits you.

ACTION

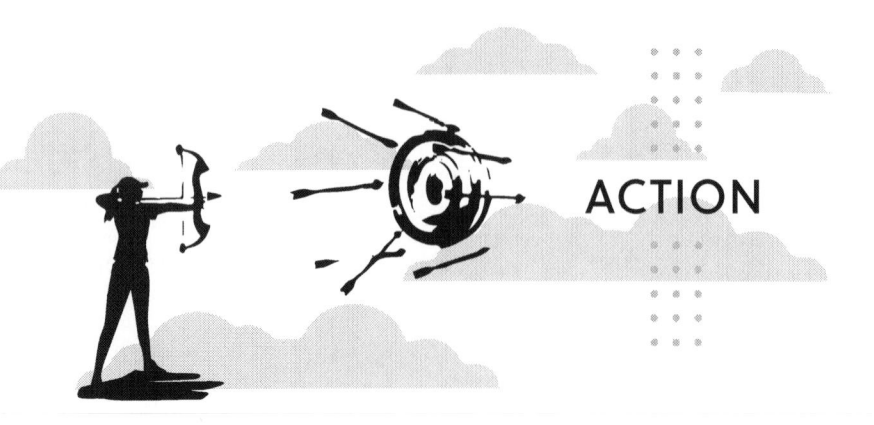

Actions to take that will drive meaningful progress

- **Get into the water** - Nobody learns swimming by just reading a book, you have to get into the water. Same applies for learning too. Work on Labs and build projects. If you are just starting, kick-off with guided lab activities and as you go deep start exploring projects and workshops.

- **Lay it out on paper first** - Whatever you are trying to build (even if it is a lab) lay it out on a paper first in form of a Design Document before going into any kind of implementation. After implementation check the end result against your design document.

- **Find your dive buddy** - There are so many forums, groups and community full of people who are ready to help. Start following the conversations happening there and you will soon find someone who may be happy to be your buddy / mentor in your exploration journey.

ALERT

Alerts to avoid common pitfalls that can hinder success

- **Outdated or faulty diving gear** - Not every practice exam may have the correct answers. Be careful while choosing practice exams. Go for only the reputed practice exams. And this applies to your training resources too. Make sure these training resources are updated and correct.

- **You can't explore the whole ocean** - Don't get overwhelmed - Be kind to yourself and stay motivated. Even if you fail any exam, you already have a lot of depth on the skills so don't be discouraged and try again. You will succeed.

- **Don't ignore fundamental knowledge** - no building can stand tall without a solid foundation. It may be an arduous task initially but ignoring fundamentals will leave you teetering like a Jenga tower. Knowing the fundamentals will take you a long way.

The Accelerators

Force multipliers for technology and Cloud explorers

They equip aspirants to soar in the Cloud and related technologies by elevating key competencies. They help multitude of followers in their rapid career progression through advocating and imparting crucial skills and knowledge.

The Accelerators

The Accelerators

Nana Janashia
Founder,
TechWorld with Nana

13 From Self Taught Software Engineer,
    To Educating Aspirants in Cloud DevOps

Mumshad Mannambeth
Founder & CEO,
KodeKloud

14 Through Courses and Trainings
    Helping Engineers Kode in Cloud

From Self Taught Software Engineer, To Educating Aspirants in Cloud DevOps

Nana Janashia
Founder,
TechWorld with Nana

Hard work, by its very nature, presents challenges and growth opportunities. The harder you work, the faster you get the desired results - if you move in the right direction. The best way to succeed is to discover what you love and then find a way to offer it to others.

Does working hard always mean you can get everything you want on the first attempt?

Nana grew up in a town near the Black Sea in Georgia, a country bordering Asia and Europe. Her mother was a housewife who stayed home to care for the family. Nana and her elder brother attended the same school growing up. She recalls how her brother was perceived as competent and intelligent, while she was seen as the troublemaker of the house. Her brother effortlessly excelled in academics, while Nana was more mischievous and free-spirited.

Curiosity to learn new things outside of one's domain opens doors to new possibilities. Young Nana Janashia learned that from her father, a civil engineer. Yet, he became curious about computers and taught himself programming in one of the early languages.

"*When my elder brother and I were little, my dad tried to teach us some computer coding concepts, but we just wanted to play games on the computer. I waited for my dad to finish studying so my brother and I could play computer games. He would tell us we had to study for an hour before we were allowed to play. Seeing him so interested in this new technology was inspiring, but we were just kids then, so we did not care much about learning it."*

"I had zero interest in learning and hoped teachers wouldn't notice me. I used to get terrible grades. But one teacher saw potential and took me under her wing, providing free private tutoring after school. She was an amazing teacher who cultivated students' potentials without expecting anything. For a couple of months, she gave me one-on-one lessons. She taught me that with effort, I could achieve anything. I quickly gained confidence, realizing I was smart as well, just like my brother. Soon, I was at the top of my class."

Nana learned her early life lesson from her teacher, that shaped her future. She could accomplish anything she set her mind to through dedication and effort. She just needed to put in enough hours and persist. From then on, she never underestimated her abilities and developed an interest in studies. What else were her interests?

Nana fondly remembers her grandfather, an entrepreneur who owned multiple businesses. He ran his office from home. His home office became Nana's playroom when he moved to a different place.

> She could accomplish anything she set her mind to through dedication and effort. She just needed to put in enough hours and persist.

She would sit in his chair and pretend to be a business person. Her grandfather's old and unneeded business documents and stamps became her favorite toys. It fuelled her childhood imagination, as she envisioned herself being a businesswoman or a lawyer one day. Will she be a successful businesswoman one day or a lawyer or someone else, probably?

"*I wanted to study business and marketing in college because of my grandfather's entrepreneurial influence. It was also interesting as business subjects are less difficult than technical engineering. I wanted to remain social and spend more time hanging out with friends rather than learning complicated subjects. My first year of college was in Georgia at an international university, and I elected Business and Marketing as my major. Then, in my second year, I won an exchange program competition fully funded by the US government* to study at a US college for one year. It was an amazing experience, getting out of my country and gaining exposure to the wider world. I studied for a year in Wisconsin, USA, and returned to Georgia."

The international exposure at a very early age was eye-opening for Nana. Contrary to the traditional path of completing her studies, she dropped out of college and opted for a job. With her newly found confidence in English as a second language, she trained aspiring students for IELTS (International English Language Testing System) and TOEFL (Test of English as a Foreign Language) exams. Her parents trusted her decision and were very supportive. She continued this for almost three years and was getting very comfortable in the role. However, she was not looking to be complacent in that position.

"I realized there wasn't much left for me to learn at my university in Georgia. And I started looking at other countries where I could continue my studies. Being able to get a student visa for Austria, I enrolled in an Austrian university and got my bachelor's degree in Business and Marketing. However, I didn't find a suitable job afterward. By this time, it was evident that getting a job in the Marketing domain was not easy. I knew I needed a company to hire me and sponsor my work visa. After consulting with a few friends and researching, I explored the technology domain instead because of the potential opportunities and growth."

In pursuit of better job prospects, Nana enrolled in the Technical College of Vienna, this time choosing to study Business Informatics. Coming from a marketing and business background, she knew pivoting to technology would be difficult. She was diving into a completely new discipline without coding experience or training.

She would have to work twice as hard as other students, primarily well-versed in IT. However, Nana was up for the challenge.

"*I vividly remember my first programming exercise - writing a simple "Hello World" program in Java. I had no idea what Java was or how to code at all. It took me three grueling hours just to write that basic program, and I still got a zero in the evaluation by the teacher because of a typo or other errors. I had one semester to catch up with classmates who had been programming for years. I was getting up at 4 am and studying till late into the evening every day, just trying to learn the fundamentals. I was no longer a person who used to hang out with friends. I had transformed into a completely different cadre.*"

Nana was going full speed on her learning journey, gaining knowledge diligently, and was determined to build a career in technology. This hard work resulted in a fruitful offer of internship as a Junior Engineer with an Austrian company while she was in her second semester. At the internship, Nana learned everything related to her assigned tasks. Even though her contract stipulated 20 hours per week because of student visa limitations, she put in 30-40 hours. Why was she overworking?

"*I was enjoying the hands-on aspect of the work. I could apply my knowledge to something more practical instead of just reading textbooks and memorizing concepts. The company only paid me a basic stipend to cover expenses, but I didn't see it as just a job. Learning as much as possible in a real-world setting was a tremendous opportunity.*"

"*Within just 3-4 months of my internship, I realized I was

learning practical skills faster on the job than in my college classes. In my Business Informatics course, there were certain subjects like CRM and ERP systems that didn't apply to programming roles. At a certain point, the ratio seemed to be ten college subjects I didn't care about versus the tangible skills I gained daily at work. So, in the third semester, I decided to drop out of college again."

This was now the second time Nana had made the bold decision to drop out of college after leaving university in Georgia a few years earlier. While some may have seen quitting multiple times as a sign of confusion or lack of direction, for Nana, it demonstrated the belief that she could chart her course. Rather than stemming from doubt, she was confident she could gain skills faster through hands-on work. For those wired to learn by doing, sometimes self-directed paths call them louder than formal credentials.

"Leaving the university also meant that I would lose my student visa, but I was confident about landing a job. Within a week of my job search, I got two full-time offers with a work permit visa sponsorship. I accepted one of the jobs, which was of a game developer, working on front-end JavaScript and graphics. The company was using an internal proprietary framework for the backend, so I had little to learn. Soon, the job became very monotonous. I was just repeating the same tasks again and again. After six months, I quit that job even though I'd lose my work permit."

Like dropping out of college multiple times before, Nana once again demonstrated the courage to diverge from convention by quitting her first full-time job without another lined up. Nana let her internal compass guide her more than external norms. This willingness to make dramatic changes to find the right fit, even without a safety net, reflected the confidence she had in herself. Where did Nana's bold confidence and willingness to take risks come from?

"It traces back to the early school experience when my teacher instilled in me the mindset that with hard work, I can achieve anything, even if it takes longer. I didn't think formal education was mandatory to get a job, especially in IT. I knew that I had to prove hands-on knowledge in my interviews. So, I focused more on gaining concrete skills. In terms of switching jobs, I think it stems from the confidence I built by constantly self-learning and taking on challenges. All the intensive self-learning gave me the confidence to take risks. I was strongly convinced I'd thrive anywhere if I put in the effort. I don't doubt my capacity to succeed in new challenges."

After quitting her first job, she applied for jobs again and waited for a few months to get a new work permit. She found a role with a company using cutting-edge technologies she was eager to learn - Docker, Microservices, IoT systems, and Mobile Apps. One of the best things that can happen for an engineer, especially early on in their career, is joining a project built from scratch. Nana got to work on a new initiative with just the proof-of-concept code. The frontend, backend, database - everything was being created brand-new. Did she get lucky to get such an opportunity?

"This experience taught me an important lesson - don't be afraid to try different jobs until you find the right fit. I wouldn't have known how unsatisfying certain roles were for me unless I spent time immersed in them. Now I know frontend/design work isn't for me, even though I initially didn't realize it. Trial and error will always *help you find where you truly thrive. You increase your chances of getting lucky when you try multiple things. I was finally learning the technologies that got me hooked."*

As a software developer on this new project, Nana worked primarily on the backend and databases, making architectural decisions since everything was being built from scratch. She enjoyed solving complex problems and being involved in the design part of the solution. Nana learned containerization skills as the application was dockerized. She liked tweaking configurations to optimize builds, tests, and releases - early exposure to DevOps-type tasks. She took an interest in the release process automation using Jenkins while her teammates focused solely on coding.

In the later phase of the project, Nana started learning new technologies - Kubernetes and AWS, out of curiosity. She convinced her managers to let her spend Fridays self-studying and working on exploratory tasks to benefit the company. With their support, she deployed their dockerized app to Kubernetes on AWS, learning tremendously by applying her skills. Though not realizing it, Nana gained valuable DevOps and cloud experience through her hands-on learning. Without formal training, she organically developed expertise in areas beyond software development that became instrumental later in her career.

> *Don't be afraid to try different jobs until you find the right fit. You increase your chances of getting lucky when you try multiple things.*

"When I joined a new project as a freelancer, they were introducing Kubernetes and needed someone with experience. I mentioned that I had worked on it before. Suddenly, everyone said, "Nana will be handling the Kubernetes part!" I became responsible for deploying and managing the Kubernetes cluster for the whole company. Stepping up and embracing Kubernetes was one of the best career decisions I made on that project. I was thrilled to have found a niche doing what I loved."

After working for a while, Nana opted to work as a contractor for another company instead of a regular employee. The prospects of getting higher pay and more flexibility compelled her to decide. Also, in some shape or form, she was giving in to the urge to be independent and start something on her own. Her dream of being a businessperson was not lost; it had just been tucked away for a while, and now it was time to materialize it.

Nana and one of her friends started working on start-up ideas besides her regular work. It served as a transitional segue as she eyed eventually going entirely into entrepreneurship. As engineers, they knew how to code and wanted to build a web application in the real estate space, an area Nana was interested in from an investment perspective.

"That first start-up attempt was a disaster, though a valuable learning experience. My friend and I fully built a real estate web application with functioning code, but the business value wasn't there. We didn't do any market validation upfront. While the venture failed, it was beneficial in technical terms. Going from zero lines of code to deploying a functioning product that people could use taught *me so much about end-to-end development. I wasn't even sad when it didn't take off business-wise. I was eager to think of the next idea and try again."*

Nana and her friend went on to experiment with a mobile app and other concepts, constantly trying out new things. They were motivated by the technical learning, not the immediate business success. That first failure showed them how to turn an idea into reality with their engineering skills. The actual viability would come later through trial and error. With each attempt, Nana further expanded her skills and knowledge. Failure wasn't something to fear, just more opportunity to learn. That's how entrepreneurs eventually get lucky - trying out different ideas relentlessly until one takes off. Which idea finally took flight for her?

"The YouTube channel, TechWorld with Nana[1], started as one of my many side projects. I noticed many experienced engineers were terrified of Kubernetes. I realized there was a need for more accessible explanations showing that Kubernetes isn't as hard as it seems. I had good notes from self-learning and setting up the production scale Kubernetes clusters. My friend and I, who worked on startup ideas together with me, decided to create a full YouTube playlist demystifying Docker and Kubernetes. With no expectation of a business, I started recording presentation-style videos explaining

> With each attempt, Nana further expanded her skills and knowledge. Failure wasn't something to fear, just more opportunity to learn.

---

[1] https://www.youtube.com/@TechWorldwithNana

the basics visually and uploaded them to YouTube in October 2019. It was an educational passion project and creative outlet in my spare time - not an intentional startup. I never imagined it would become more.

At first, Nana and her friend were not thinking of it as a business, but within the first couple of months, they saw strong interest and engagement. Still, Nana didn't consider herself a YouTuber - she saw herself as an engineer who wanted to build a real startup. They sat down and agreed that the channel was gaining traction effortlessly, so they should turn it into an official startup. They first tried sponsored videos, securing one partnership. However, chasing sponsorships wasn't very exciting for Nana.

There was a clear moment when our YouTube channel started taking off. For the first couple of months, we had diligently posted weekly videos. Then YouTube's algorithm noticed our consistency and started actively promoting our content. One day, our Prometheus monitoring video was featured on users' homepages. We obsessively tracked the analytics and saw the views suddenly spiked into the thousands per day. That video alone hit over 100k views. Then, our Terraform video got the same treatment. We realized we could combine the most popular videos into a structured course. That became our first "Zero to Hero" course on Kubernetes, with 4 hours of video lessons. That course made the channel explode and hit 100K subscribers.

Nana wanted to leverage the demand for her explainer-style content more innovatively than typical YouTube monetization models. That's when she conceived the idea for an entire DevOps bootcamp - a complete educational program taking beginners to be job-ready as DevOps engineers. She could not find similar bootcamp offerings in 2020, so it was tremendously challenging to figure everything out from scratch.

With only a few reference points, Nana had to scope the entire curriculum herself - which technologies to teach, in what order, and the overall syllabus. The ambitious scope of the DevOps boot camp focused on the most popular tools and platforms like Docker, Kubernetes, AWS, and Terraform excited Nana. She was driven by the chance to create something truly unique and fulfill an untapped need. The bootcamp allowed her to leverage her content more innovatively, aligning with her entrepreneurial vision. Nana focused on three pillars - bootcamps, courses, and YouTube videos. The quality and usefulness of her content helped achieve steady linear growth for the YouTube channel in both subscribers and views. As of November 2023, only four years after uploading her first explainer video, Nana now has over 900,000 YouTube subscribers.

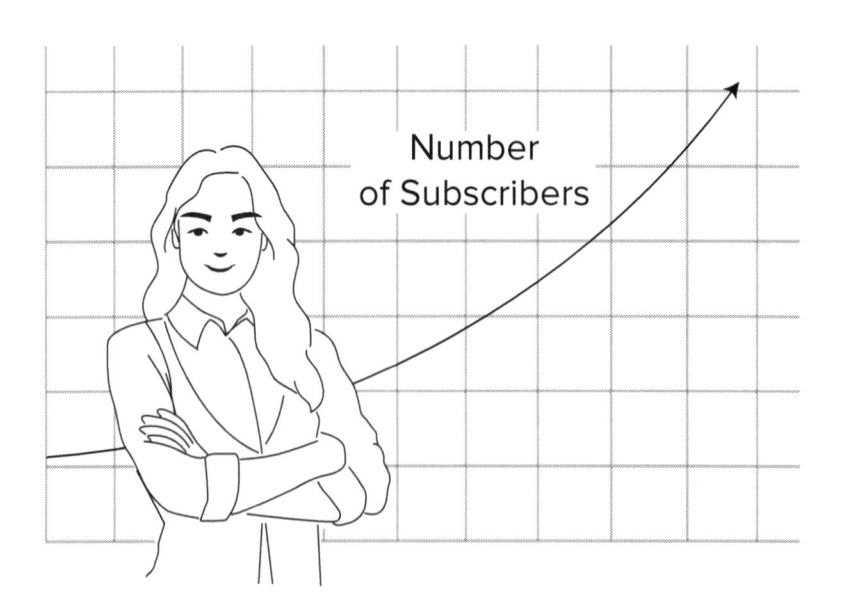

"While still shocked at our channel's sudden growth, I got a surprising email one day - Docker wanted to name me a Docker Captain[1]. Soon after, AWS also contacted me, with several of their teams nominating me to become an AWS Hero[2] for my container and cloud videos. The ultimate validation was getting endorsed by the top cloud provider because they valued my tutorials. The CNCF Ambassador title also followed. More than viewers complimenting the videos, being sought out by Docker, AWS, CNCF - the experts in these technologies - proved I was creating high-quality, helpful educational content. It's fulfilling when industry leaders recognize your work. This unexpected early support pushed me to strive to produce the best learning resources possible."

Nana is on track to cross 1 million subscribers, a significant milestone. She plans to celebrate this achievement with her community, who have enabled her success through their viewership and support. For an independent creator, hitting seven digits reflects the value her content provides to aspiring technology professionals worldwide. Nana built this engaged audience by reliably publishing educational videos for free on YouTube. That credibility and trust enabled her paid offerings like bootcamps to succeed. With nearly 1 million people relying on her tutorials, Nana has established herself as a leading instructor shaping the next generation of tech talent.

* * *

Nana's journey shows how - believing in yourself, hard work, curiosity, and a willingness to take risks can open up new avenues of

---

[1] https://www.docker.com/captains/nana-janashia/
[2] https://aws.amazon.com/developer/community/heroes/nana-janashia/

opportunity. Initially trained in Business Studies and Marketing, she pivoted her career multiple times and proactively learned emerging technologies like Kubernetes and AWS cloud. Nana let her interests guide her rather than sticking to a predefined role.

For aspiring entrepreneurs, Nana emphasizes starting small by validating ideas through real-world experiments. Don't be intimidated to turn a passion project into a profession once you see it gaining traction. Stay relentlessly curious and always be learning. With the right mindset and persistence, unforeseen doors can open through the things you do simply for the joy and challenge.

ADVICE

Advice when following a Cloud career path

- **Self-Analysis** - Identify your strengths to help you select the most suitable role for you. For example, if you enjoy working on abstract concepts, design or architecting roles will probably be appropriate. A programming or operations role will suit you better if you want to acquire specialized skills.

- **Be receptive** - Whether a seasoned professional or a novice, stay open to new ideas from various sources and inputs. Technology changes quickly, so be receptive to further knowledge, methods, trends, and inspiration even if you have mastered it all.

- **Everything can be learned** - With dedication and hard work, everything can be learned. Learn from mistakes, consider alternative viewpoints, adjust your path, and adapt a learning mindset. Considers every new experience as an opportunity to learn.

ACTION

Actions to take that will drive meaningful progress

- **Set your objectives** - At the beginning of every week, month, or year, set goals for yourself. This should give you a clear view of what needs to be done. When identifying these targets, ensure they are realistic, time-bound, and measurable.

- **Fail early, fail fast** - Failing may not be seen as a positive outcome, but it can provide valuable life lessons. Through experimentation, figure out beforehand what you don't like and what you like. You can use failure as an opportunity to reconsider your approach and avoid repeating previous mistakes.

- **Project-based learning** - Instead of passive listening and memorization, build a project to reinforce and showcase your skills. Acquire a more profound knowledge through active exploration of real-world challenges and problems.

ALERT

Alerts to avoid common pitfalls that can hinder success

- **Not being focused** - You learn much faster and more accurately when attention is focused, for some time, on one thing at a time. Don't give in to the urge to juggle, multitask, and engage in other forms of "attention shifting;" stay focused. Your focus shapes your life.

- **Not being persistent** - Persistence is essential to success; the more you display, the more you accomplish. Ultimately, persistence will differentiate you and allow you to maximize your ability. Don't dream of wild success and recognition overnight. It takes time and persistence.

- **Staying in the comfort zone** - The comfort zone is a silent killer. It gets in the way of your professional growth and personal growth. Gradually expand it and earn the countless rewards waiting at the end of your comfort zone.

Pathfinders Undefeated Progressives Liberators **Accelerators** Pinnacles

Through Courses and Trainings Helping Engineers Kode in Cloud

14

Mumshad Mannambeth
Founder & CEO,
KodeKloud

If you want to learn something, read about it.
If you want to understand something, write about it.
If you want to master something, teach it.

Was teaching technology to more than a million learners easy?

Growing up in a beautiful town in Kannur located in Kerala, the southern part of India - Mumshad enjoyed spending time with his family. His father worked as a Sales Representative in a petroleum company in Saudi Arabia, away from home. His father managed to get the family there to stay with him for a year. *That* was a defining moment for Mumshad.

"I was ten at that time. I got enrolled in the school there and was awestruck by the quality of education and the facilities. I wished to continue studying there for the rest of my school life. At the end of the year, when it was time for us to return to India, I requested my father to allow me to stay. After some hesitation, he agreed. So, I continued living with my father in Saudi Arabia while my mother and the other siblings returned to India. I lived there until I was 15."

Mumshad was enjoying his newfound freedom. When his father would go to work, he would be out most of the time, roam freely, and meet others in his age group. He spent a lot of time exploring and playing outdoors. The scorching sun in Saudi Arabia did not affect his playful spirit. This was also the time which shaped his life.

"*I was a below-average student until I was ten. My move to Saudi Arabia changed something. In my five years there, I progressed from a below-average student to one of the bright ones in my class. In India, my class had about 60 students. I never made it in the top 20. Here, my class had 30 students, and in one of the exams, I was in the top 10. Though I was at the 10th position, it was still a great feeling.*"

Mumshad had tasted some academic success for the first time and was proud of it. He realized that if he could come this far despite putting in minimal effort, imagine how far he could go with focused efforts. He befriended others at the top of the list and learned how they studied and followed a similar approach. He was among the top 2 in the class by the end of his academic year.

While in Saudi Arabia, he requested his father to get him a computer at home as some of his friends had it. After months of persuasion, his father got him one. Like a typical teenager, he used the computer primarily to play games rather than study. He was hooked on strategy games and spent hours and hours playing. He had figured out ways to fix the computer when it broke and hack his way through getting the games to work. Was this the reason he picked computer science as a field of study?

"*I had a computer since I was 11 years old and thought I was *good at it. After returning to India, I joined a 3-year computer science diploma course at a college in Bangalore. I did not understand programming initially, but I picked it eventually after helping my friends debug their code in the lab. Once I had gotten the basics, I spent time learning more independently and was way beyond the curriculum taught at my college."*

Mumshad vividly remembers his first year in college and being a topper of his batch. He was also confident about continuing with the same momentum in the later years of college, but that was far from reality. He did not do that well in the remaining years of his college, and his grades dropped by the time he completed the three-year diploma. Probably, his focus got distracted as he started enjoying college life. What's next?

"I joined Wipro Technologies right after I completed my diploma through a campus placement. I worked in their technical support department. Although my salary was a meager amount, as an 18-year-old, I was happy to earn money. The company provided transportation and food on-site, and by doing night shifts, one could make some extra cash, so I ended up doing a lot of night shifts."

Mumshad worked at Wipro for less than two years and moved to HP in a similar technical support role, supporting customers with storage systems-related issues. While this role provided him with domain knowledge and a learning opportunity, he sought a more operations-centric role. Did he choose the next job carefully?

"I selected jobs based on different aspects at different career stages depending on what I felt was important to me then. In the

early days, I simply looked at how big the company was and how big of a salary hike I was offered. Eventually, I realized I should prioritize the experience I'd get working on the project over anything else. So, I started focusing on the work I'd be doing when I picked new roles."

Mumshad quickly learned about different aspects of his work and started exploring things beyond his daily activities. He constantly looked for opportunities to learn and upskill himself. He realized that not everything is under your control and to accept things for what they are, especially when working in a corporate environment.

"I wasn't the rebel type. If I didn't like something, I walked away from it. If I didn't get the opportunity I deserved, I'd walk away from it. I later realized how important it is to have conversations to share my views and work things out."

Mumshad also sought roles and skills to help him migrate to a different country. He was looking to get global exposure and also experience different cultures. When the right opportunity showed up, Mumshad seized it.

"I spent two years at HP and switched to EMC to a more System Operations role. During this stint, I realized there was a huge potential to automate many mundane operational tasks, and it was time to put on my developer hat. I created multiple tools to help automate storage migrations, design solutions for storage systems, and many more."

> 💡 *I later realized how important it is to have conversations to share my views and work things out.*

Once the word got around about the tools he had created, Mumshad got global exposure within the company. Trusting his abilities, EMC offered him a role in the US. He was assigned to the team looking to automate the deployment of a Hybrid Cloud Environment using the VMware virtualization suite of products. There were lots of expectations from him to successfully deliver this project. Suddenly, the stakes had become invariably high.

"*It was a steep learning curve. I worked tirelessly for long hours as I learned completely new technologies. That was the first time I was introduced to the cloud and DevOps technologies. After much effort, we reduced the time to put the private cloud stack together from a few months to a day - 18 hours or so, to be precise. We used Ansible as the automation framework and Docker to package the solution itself.*"

During this time, Mumshad was introduced to the AWS cloud platform. He set a target to learn it and started preparing for the AWS Certified Cloud Practitioner Certification. Mumshad was entering a new technical domain unbeckoned to the fact that this would change his career trajectory.

```
DOCKERFILE

FROM alpine
CMD ["echo", "Hello Leaner! This is the start of a new journey."]
```

Certifications give you a targe, especially for those who haven't had the opportunity to work in a Cloud environment and are trying to validate their skills to qualify for job switches.

"*I've used certifications to get better jobs in my early career days. I would use it to prove that even though I have not had much experience in that space, I've put in the time and effort to learn and get certified. I think that's the most important aspect of a certification.*"

He went on a learning spree and explored product documents, Udemy video courses, and other resources. While this was happening, he started a new thread in parallel.

"*One day, while preparing for the AWS Certified Cloud Practitioner certification through online learning platforms, I saw a "Teach with us" button. I have always enjoyed teaching. I'd imagine teaching someone whenever I learned something new. It helped me look at things from a different perspective and do the research needed to learn things thoroughly to simplify things and explain them well to others.*"

Success is never an overnight endeavor. It takes persistence, focus, hard work, and, most of all, love for what you are doing. He was encouraged by the thought of creating a course and publishing it. He quickly put together a course on Excel formulas for beginners. Unfortunately, nobody bought it as there were 1000s of other Excel

> *I've used certifications to get better jobs in my early career days. I would use it to prove that even though I have not had much experience in that space, I've put in the time and effort to learn and get certified.*

courses on Udemy at that time.

"Through this experiment, I realized that there is a demand for content, but not on general topics. People are looking to learn the coveted skills, the next big things. So, I thought, why not create courses for something else I know? Maybe a course on DevOps tools that covers Ansible, Docker, and Kubernetes."

Mumshad could not find many courses out there on these DevOps technologies. He was also inspired by the many coding platforms that taught people to code interactively, but there was no interactive platform for DevOps. He sensed that this could be a niche area he should explore. It was an opportunity to build something new.

"I needed a domain name for my website. I wanted it to be short and just two words max. I planned to create courses to teach people how to code cloud-native applications. From that, I derived code cloud. The original domain name - codecloud.com, was available but priced very high. So, I swapped the C for the K (for Kubernetes) and purchased that domain for $10."

```
docker-compose.yml

services:
   myservice:
      image: www.kodekloud.com
      ports:
         - "80:80"
```

It was still a side project to satisfy his urge to teach and help people learn complex topics. On the job front, Mumshad was climbing the corporate ladder and assisting the customers in their Cloud, DevOps, and automation journey. Instead of just implementation and troubleshooting, he designed solutions for private and public cloud customers. It was time for another change.

"*After working in the US for three years, I had an opportunity to move into a Solutions Architect role in the DevOps space in Singapore. I was also looking for a move closer to India, which worked well. I left EMC and joined World Wide Technology as a Senior Cloud Automation Engineer. I helped customers through end-to-end project lifecycle, from conducting POCs to designing and implementing solutions.*"

Though his stint in the US ended, his content creation journey was just starting. Mumshad's first course on DevOps was well-received by learners. Through the feedback provided by the learners, he knew he was on the right track. But were there any challenges?

"*There have been a lot of ups and downs since publishing my first course, but I've always managed to stay focused. Also, the biggest factor in KodeKloud's success has been word of mouth. Our students have been recommending the quality of our courses to others, and that's been the biggest driver of growth. I listened to students and built a product around what they love and what is trending in the industry. Our most popular content has been our Kubernetes courses.*"

While Mumshad worked in Singapore, his content business took off. He prioritized collecting inputs from the existing learners on what they wanted to learn next. It was time to do what he loved the most. He quit his job and focused all his energy and efforts on scaling KodeKloud.

> **DOCKER COMMAND**
> docker run -d www.kodekloud.com sleep infinity

Mumshad knew it wouldn't be a walk in the park, and he was prepared for it. He never had a second thought to return to his corporate job again. He listened to the student feedback, gauged the market demand, and pushed himself to make the learning journey easier for others. What kind of challenges did he face while scaling KodeKloud?

"*I started as a one-person army creating one course, and now we have 70+ team members, helping more than a million learners through 80+ courses. Scaling to this level was not easy. There have been different challenges at different stages of the company. I followed the "Keep calm and build on" mindset to push through all the problems of building a company.*"

While scaling KodeKloud, Mumshad faced battles on three fronts – People, Process, and Technology.

People Challenge – The initial challenge was going from an individual to a team. It was difficult to find the right people who shared the same vision and onboarding them.

Solution – "*This was probably the hardest challenge. I realized

I had to do most of the sourcing, interviewing & hiring by myself. I was posting jobs on LinkedIn and AngelList and directly contacting potential candidates. Platforms like Upwork and Toptal helped hire people for short-term requirements. We made many mistakes in the early years, but I got a little better after much practice."

Process Challenge – While scaling, maintaining the top quality of the content and practice labs was crucial.

Solution – *"We built a team of expert instructional designers, video editors, quality assurance people, and project managers who coordinated with trainers to ensure all courses were of high quality. We also made sure we carefully created fewer higher quality courses and have a crazy focus on quality rather than quantity."*

Technology Challenge – Keeping the lab's platform secure from hackers and handling peak traffic, especially during the sale period, was difficult. It was a constant challenge.

Solution – *"Our lab engineering team is responsible for maintaining and scaling the labs and ensuring security measures are implemented to prevent attacks. We use an isolated sandboxed runtime that provides additional security to the virtual lab environments. We have rules configured so any attack is flagged, and the attacker is blocked from our systems."*

Mumshad diligently and tirelessly worked to scale the KodeKloud platform, helping millions of learners. But did he seek mentorship at any point

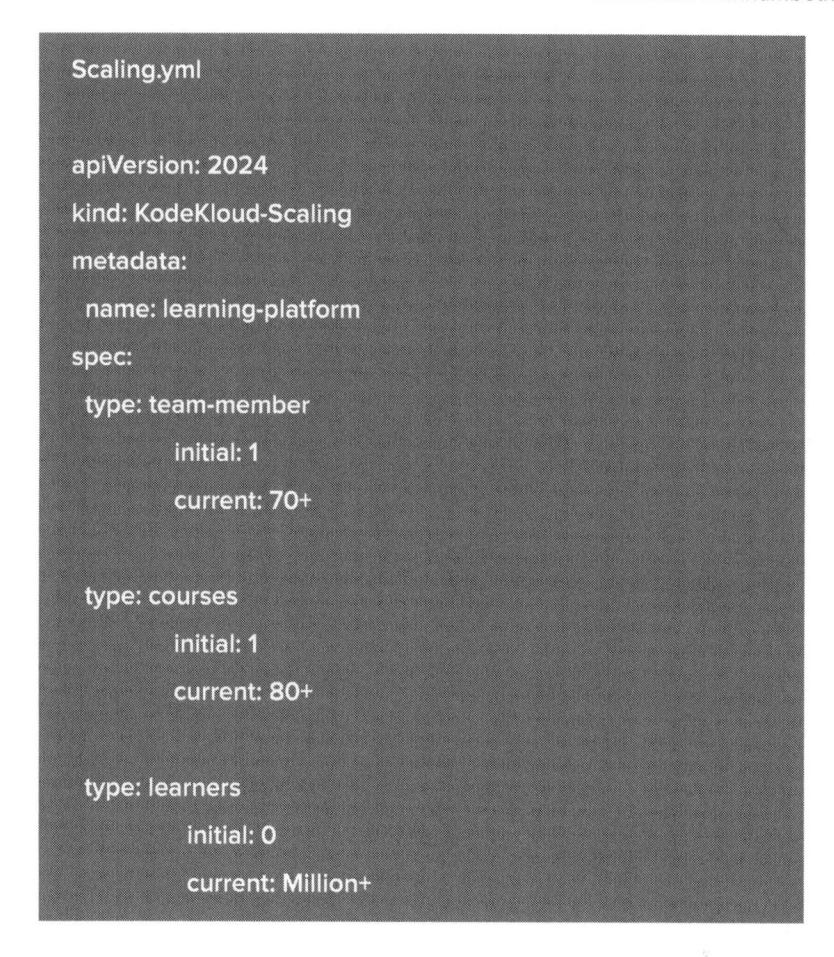

```yaml
Scaling.yml

apiVersion: 2024
kind: KodeKloud-Scaling
metadata:
  name: learning-platform
spec:
  type: team-member
      initial: 1
      current: 70+

  type: courses
      initial: 1
      current: 80+

  type: learners
      initial: 0
      current: Million+
```

"*I do have a few mentors that I speak to from time to time. I think it's imperative, especially when doing things you haven't done before. I often feel like I have no clue about certain things, and that's when mentors can be a good resource to reach out to. At other times, they are a good sounding board for new ideas.*"

While helping others learn about technology, he has not let the learner in him get sidetracked. He regularly reaches out to others in a similar situation as he is or has done better and tries to learn how they achieved success. Just as he puts it, *learning is a continued process.*

Mumshad plans to continue building KodeKloud as the go-to platform for learning anything related to DevOps, Linux, Cloud, and Cloud Native technologies. He thrives on providing real-time environment to learners so they can gain hands-on experience by working on trending IT technologies.

This Arsenal fan lives by the quote from "The Diary of a CEO"

Those who hoard gold have riches for a moment.
Those who hoard knowledge and skills have riches for a lifetime.

ADVICE

Advice when following a Cloud career path

- **Continuous Learning** - The cloud tech landscape is constantly evolving. Keep up with the latest in Kubernetes, Docker, Ansible, Terraform, and emerging technologies.

- **Hands-On Experience** - Hands-on projects solidify learning and are impressive on resumes. Whether through personal projects, internships, or job roles, getting hands-on with cloud technologies is vital.

- **Find your passion** - Look for the job you enjoy doing soon. If you are stuck in a job that doesn't resonate with your love, find something better and then quit. Do not quit first and be without a job.

ACTION

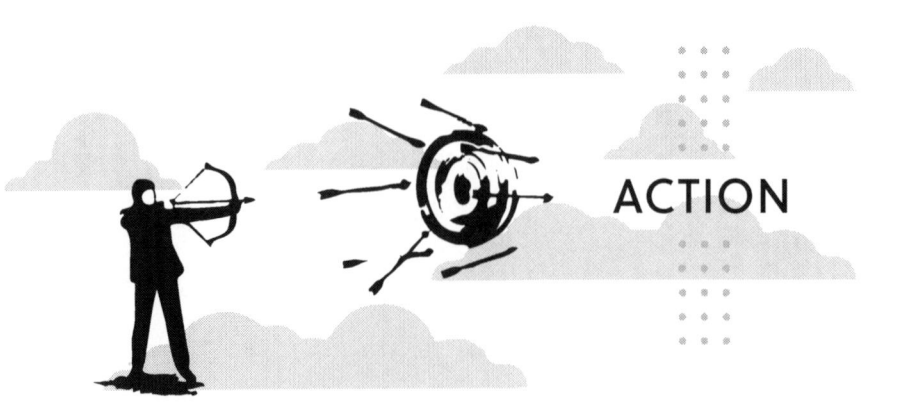

Actions to take that will drive meaningful progress

- **Join Technical user groups and meetups** - Find local user groups, events, and meetups to connect with people in person. This not only helps in learning from others' experiences but also in building your professional network.

- **Get Certified** - Pursue relevant certifications in AWS, Kubernetes, or Terraform. Certifications validate your skills and are often highly regarded in the industry.

- **Embrace Project - Based learning from the start**: Work on real-world projects at every stage of your learning journey. This could be anything from deploying a simple app using Docker to setting up a Kubernetes cluster.

ALERT

Alerts to avoid common pitfalls that can hinder success

- **Avoiding Fundamentals** - Don't jump into advanced topics without a solid understanding of the basics. Ensure you have a strong foundation in core concepts before moving to more complex technologies.

- **Overlooking Soft Skills** - Technical skills are crucial, but soft skills like communication, teamwork, and problem-solving are often underestimated. A lack of these skills can hinder progression in a career.

- **Being impatient** - Transitioning to a cloud career takes time. Focus your efforts in the right direction, and you will be successful eventually. Keep calm and build

The Pinnacles

At the apex of Cloud success

Through expertise and tireless drive, they've mastered the immense challenges on the path to the peak. Their journeys show others the route to reach the Cloud computing heights.

The Pinnacles

The Pinnacles

Ryan Kroonenburg
Founder,
A Cloud Guru

15 Assisted People Migrate Countries, Helping Millions Transition to Cloud

Jeff Barr
Vice President and Chief Evangelist, AWS

16 For J = 1 to AWS

Pinnacles

Assisted People Migrate Countries, Helping Millions Transition to Cloud

Ryan Kroonenberg
Founder,
A Cloud Guru

Growth is never easy, and it's even more complicated if you are thinking about hypergrowth. This doesn't mean that it is impossible, but does hypergrowth just happen, or does it have to be achieved?

Let's explore the case with the hypergrowth of A Cloud Guru – the training platform that helped millions of learners transition to the Cloud.

Message from the Authors

Even though every journey in the book traces a unique path, they all have one persistent thread - *continuous learning*. Frankly, that was unsurprising, as a learning mindset is essential in every aspect of life. However, there was another common theme that we noticed. Most of them started learning cloud using *A Cloud Guru*, a.k.a. Ryan Kroonenburg's courses. The same is true for us, the authors of this book, as we also started our *cloud learning* journey watching to Ryan's videos.

As the vast majority of the people in the cloud industry got upskilled using Ryan's courses, we thought our readers would be interested in knowing how Ryan started his cloud career journey. We knew it was a very long shot to reach out to Ryan and ask him to share his story for the book. It was a long shot, indeed! However, we persisted; we kept chasing Ryan till we got his attention. When he finally saw our message, he humbly replied, *"I would love to be involved with your project and share my journey if it is not too late?"* We were delighted to get his response. We scheduled time with him and had a lengthy interview to understand his larger-than-life story. He candidly shared his life lessons, setbacks, challenges, and successes.

Buckle up, readers; next is the story, not just of "A Cloud Guru" but of "The Cloud Guru..."

Destiny is not defined by where you are born but is ultimately shaped by our choices. Our place of birth sets the starting line but not necessarily the finish line. You could be born in the most isolated corner of the world yet still set your sights on space travel within your lifetime. And it could not be truer for Ryan Kroonenberg, who was born and raised in the remote outback of Western Australia. His father owned a truck stop business there during Ryan's early childhood.

When Ryan turned six, his father sold the truck stop and moved the family to Adelaide in South Australia. After Ryan's parents divorced, he and his younger brother Sam lived with their father. Their mother worked full-time in human resources at a university but remained involved in raising them by residing nearby. After settling in Adelaide, Ryan's father started a new business selling computers and opened one of the early computer stores in South Australia.

"My brother Sam and I had access to three or four computers in our house, enough for us to set up LAN parties and play computer games like King's Quest and Space Quest. I learned how to type while trying to solve the King's Quest game. I got introduced to computers early on in life, but at the time, there was no vision of programming in sight. It was all about gaming."

Though Ryan has access to computers from an early age, reading opened up new worlds for him as a young boy. One day, he discovered Issac Asimov's *The Bicentennial Man* and became engrossed by the idea of robots. He loved watching shows like Transformers and Voltron, captivated by their robotic characters. The sci-fi books of Arthur C. Clarke fueled Ryan's imagination, too, making him want to be an astronaut and experience zero gravity in space (a dream that would become reality for him in time, as described later). One might assume that an avid reader like Ryan would excel at school. But was he a dedicated student during his upbringing?

"I would only study enough to meet the minimum grade requirements to get into university. I focused more on having a good time than being a top student. I was a laid-back teenager, but I realized I had to rely on myself for my future. The fear of failure always kept me from getting too sidetracked. I knew I needed a degree and build a career to support myself. With that understanding, my attitude toward education improved when I finally got to university. I started studying to learn things."

After some time in Adelaide, Ryan's family gravitated back to Perth in Western Australia. His father ran a successful computer store and worked as an accountant, pulling Ryan toward the same career trajectory. Like a satellite in his father's orbit, Ryan agreed to follow that path, enrolling in a double degree program in Accounting and Finance at Curtin University. Though firmly grounded in his studies, Ryan still felt moments of weightlessness, his mind drifting to worlds far beyond the ledger books. He aspired to explore alien worlds, seeking adventures where accountants might only dare to dream.

"I was very interested in moving to London after I finished my studies for better career prospects as an accountant. I had a plan but was unsure if it would work out, so I also thought of a Plan B - if I had trouble finding work or if my accounting career didn't pan out in London, I could always help people get visas to immigrate to Australia. I knew many British people wanted to immigrate to Australia then, and there were very few immigration consultants in the UK then. So, with that in mind, I enrolled in a postgraduate diploma program in Immigration Law before I moved to London. I studied diligently and completed the degree ahead of schedule."

He had a failsafe mechanism now of being an immigration consultant if not an accountant. If job prospects fizzled like a failed launch, Ryan had a backup booster ready to fire. Fuelled by his vision and knowledge, he was ready to blast off on an arcing path to the UK.

> *My attitude toward education improved when I finally got to university. I started studying to learn things.*

"*After moving to London, I got a job with an insurance company doing actuarial work - some of the most tedious accounting and finance calculations you can imagine. One of my first tasks was calculating statistical odds for insurance policies, which was incredibly boring. I started writing Visual Basic macros to automate many repetitive processes to break out from the boring manual tasks. I learned scripting, which interested me in Tech, but I lasted there only for a year.*"

Ryan found the repetitive calculations at the insurance company to be as dull as drifting through space without thrust. He yearned to break free of this mundane orbit. He recalled his postgraduate diploma in immigration law - the backup booster he had prepared. Ryan launched a newspaper ad, offering his services in helping people immigrate to Australia. He arranged the money for the newspaper ad by maxing out his credit card limit. Too big of a gamble. Isn't it?

"*I was nervous that I had just made a big mistake taking out the £5000 newspaper ad and that I'd be paying it off for months. But that ad generated around 22 clients for me, each paying a couple thousand pounds for immigration help in getting to Australia. I realized there was no need to keep working at an insurance company crunching numbers when I could instead be doing something I loved - helping people immigrate to Australia.*"

The single ad fuelled his career's escape velocity, instantly paying for itself. It sparked Ryan's maiden entrepreneurial launch, setting his startup on an unexpected growth path. At just 24, he began ferrying hopeful emigrants to Australia. Within three years, his company rapidly expanded into a soaring enterprise, ballooning to over 150 employees worldwide. He established orbital offices in London, Vancouver, Cape Town, Barcelona, and Australia to support operations. He was accelerating at light speed.

This Big Bang expansion introduced a lot of operational challenges in terms of coordinating various government systems. Ryan enlisted the help of technology and built automated systems for immigration application management. His approach was to automate lots of paperwork by integrating with government systems through APIs. He enjoyed this approach of automation through technology. Little did he know that this interest would be of utmost importance later in his life.

"*My first startup grew massively and much faster than I anticipated. I was highly qualified in immigration law - licensed to practice in Australia, Canada, and the UK. I was probably among the only globally registered across all three jurisdictions. So, there was a huge demand for my services. Then, the financial crisis hit in 2008, and the system collapsed. To move countries, most people sold their houses first to arrange a substantial amount of funds, but during the financial crisis, house prices plummeted by a third, and there were no buyers. At the same time, Australia and Canada tightened immigration to protect local jobs."*

His business got absorbed in the gravity well of an economic black hole. Practically overnight, demand evaporated for Ryan's previously in-high-demand immigration law expertise. Even his qualifications, once rare as a moon rock, were useless asteroid debris. Will he be able to sustain the startup?

As revenue dried up, Ryan painfully laid off employees, even his mother, who had joined the company. Eventually, the money ran out entirely, and Ryan had to shut down the once high-flying operation. He now faced starting over to find new opportunities, having guided his first bold entrepreneurial venture from meteoric rise to heartbreaking demise. It was time to pull the handle on the ejection seat.

"With my immigration business shut down, I needed to transition into a new industry. I got into Tech while building the integration system for immigration work - learning PHP, MySQL, database design, web servers, and more. So, I decided to switch careers and get into IT fully. I attended night school to earn MCSE (Microsoft Certified Systems Engineer) and CCNA (Cisco Certified Network Associate) certifications. I got a job doing first-line tech support for a homeless charity in London, but it wasn't exactly a "proper" tech job."

After earning his certifications, Ryan landed a job as a Systems Engineer at Rackspace in 2010. His ability to solve business problems helped him to see the holistic picture, and he soon moved into a Solutions Architect role.

Seeking more significant challenges, Ryan switched jobs and landed an Infrastructure Architect role at SunGard Availability Systems. At SunGard, Ryan worked with hundreds of servers across multiple data centers, implementing MPLS networking, disaster recovery systems, and failover between sites.

"*I was learning quickly as an Infrastructure Architect, but when I learned about AWS and Cloud technology, I knew it would make traditional infrastructure roles obsolete. I realized my job administering physical servers won't be relevant within five years as companies will migrate to the Cloud. The demand would be for Cloud Architects. After finally breaking into the tech industry, I feared falling behind the curve again if I didn't adapt fast enough. So, I decided to get myself AWS certified.*"

Ryan started his AWS certifications journey in December 2014 with AWS Certified Solutions Architect Associate certification. At the time, there were no online courses or comprehensive training materials. A few online platforms existed, but no one had yet created in-depth AWS video courses. The only option was expensive in-person classroom training. Not only was the cost prohibitive, but

> When I learned about AWS and Cloud technology, I knew it would make traditional infrastructure roles obsolete.

people also had to take multiple days off work to attend. Even then, the classes only covered high-level concepts, not the hands-on knowledge needed for the certification.

"I read through all the whitepapers, experimented in the AWS Management Console, and used Reddit to learn from others' experiences. It was a scramble, piecing together information wherever I could find it. I started creating slide decks to help memorize everything for the AWS exam. One day, while making the slides, I had an idea - if I passed this exam, I should create an online course since nobody had done it yet. It seemed like a great way to earn side income."

"All this while, I switched jobs and worked on AWS technologies briefly. I had also been interviewing for a Solutions Architect role at AWS. I went through their process twice but got rejected both times. In hindsight, those two missed opportunities were a blessing in disguise. If I had landed that AWS job right away, I may never have explored building an online training business."

Ryan began recording an AWS course, narrating his slide decks with no face on camera - essentially lecturing to himself. He launched the raw course just before taking the exam, not knowing if he would pass or fail. Ryan sat for the exam in January 2015. When he found out he had passed, he raced to update the course, adding all the essential facts fresh from his memory.

"It was crazy - I had no money back then, a new baby at home, and could barely afford a £40 microphone to record with the course. I worried I'd never earn back that £40 investment. But within two *weeks, the course brought in $2000 - enough to buy proper recording gear and a new laptop!"*

That humble course launch was the beginning of an online cloud learning platform. His first certification and video course was for AWS Certified Solutions Architect Associate, followed by AWS Certified Developer Associate and AWS Certified Sysops Administrator Associate. The demand was staggering; within 4-5 months, Ryan earned $100,000 monthly from these courses. He saw Cloud computing as a new galaxy to probe.

"*With no platform back then, I published my courses on Udemy. The revenue was split between Udemy and me. This got me thinking - having my platform to sell the courses would be more beneficial. With that goal in mind, I reached out to my brother Sam, who was working as a software engineer in Melbourne, Australia. I pitched Sam my idea for building our online cloud learning platform."*

The countdown for the next reentry mission in the entrepreneurial domain had begun. Ryan came up with the name A Cloud Guru (ACG) and charted the course for a new venture. His brother Sam, whose engineering talents could launch ACG's technological infrastructure, joined him on this ambitious Cloud mission. Though separated by time zones, the two began constructing their galactic platform. A successful space mission requires a lot of coordination between the command module and the service module. The brothers knew that banding together could create something greater than the sum of their strengths.

"*When Sam was convinced to build ACG, he took a four-week*

leave from work, his entire annual leave. Luckily, AWS Lambda had just been released, so Sam built ACG on the new serverless framework. The huge advantage of serverless was that we'd only incur compute costs when a user invoked a function. So, we could essentially bootstrap the platform for free, using AWS's 12-month free tier, and only pay for usage from paying customers. There were hardly any running costs."

While Sam was developing ACG's platform, Ryan continued advancing his AWS certifications. He achieved the AWS Certified Solutions Architect Professional certification and released the video courses on the newly developed ACG platform. Soon after, Ryan attained his AWS Certified DevOps Engineer Professional certification but did not have time to create a course. With his focus on growing ACG, he hired other instructors to develop courses for the AWS Certified DevOps Engineer Professional certification and AWS Specialty certifications. But how did he maintain the quality of the courses while ACG was expanding? How was he able to handle the quality attenuation?

"I had made a cheat sheet for the new instructors to adhere to. The basic formula was to teach in a way a five-year-old could understand. The teaching should not feel like you're reading a script. It should be interesting and engaging. Also, I used to refine it constantly. When we had just started, each session was 20 minutes, but then we reduced it to 10 minutes. After every session, a revision was provided, and after all the sections, exam tips were available in the review section."

Ryan and Sam had fought a lot in their childhood and may even argue today with their difference of opinion in politics and other matters, but when it came to their startup, they were a strong team with a matching wavelength. They handled different roles in ACG based on their strengths. Sam became the CEO, and Ryan focused on managing and building content for the platform. The pivotal point of ACG growth happened when they got a call from a Venture Capitalist.

A CLOUD GURU

"*At the time, I was based in the UK, and my brother Sam was in Australia. We were building ACG remotely between the two of us. Around 70-80% of our customers were in the United States, where we had zero presence. Then, one day, while I was on vacation in Italy, enjoying the stunning views of Lake Como, I got a surprising call. A venture capital firm called Elephant VC had read about us. They asked if we had considered taking an investment. I explained we didn't need money since our revenues were strong. Why take funding and dilute our ownership?*"

The VC firm made a valid point - ACG was missing a huge

market opportunity without a base in the US, their largest customer geography. Their call awakened Ryan to the need for boots on the ground in the US to continue ACG's velocity vector.

This was the start of Phase 2 in ACG's growth. Ryan and Sam met with Elephant VC and raised their first funding. Though unplanned, they recognized a seasoned VC as a co-pilot could help steer ACG to new heights. Once funded, ACG wasted no time establishing a footprint in the US. After scoping several locations, they chose Austin, Texas, for its talent pool and lower operating costs.

Within a few years, Ryan and Sam had built a thriving mission control hub. From those scrappy early days, ACG's crew grew into a 500-strong team across the globe. With a solid US foundation, ACG was cleared for the next leg in their boundless journey.

"*It was time for ACG to become Cloud agnostic since we knew Amazon would eventually make their own free online learning platform - potentially destroying our business. We realized no one was offering vendor-neutral cloud training covering multiple platforms. So, we started teaching Azure, Google Cloud, Linux, Red Hat, and more. It was all about mitigating risk and not relying too heavily on one cloud vendor or certification track.*"

While ACG was going omnidirectional, another growth area for them was tie-ups with big enterprises to upskill their workforce. ACG started using a B2C (business-to-customer) model, focused solely on individual consumers. Their first B2B (business-to-business) customer was Capital One, a giant Financial Corporation that wanted to train a large part of their workforce on AWS technologies.

"*Drew Firment worked at Capital One then and was involved in this process. However, investors encouraged us to build a B2B business after Series A funding funding by creating a sales team to structure large enterprise deals. That's when Drew came and joined us to help build our B2B sales division. He is still with the company today. He is an AWS hero and a very good friend of mine.*"

As ACG's popularity skyrocketed, they had a friendly rival in fellow Texas-based Linux Academy. Like twin stars, both platforms shone bright with stellar products, and their user bases were often playfully competitive on Reddit.

"*Linux Academy was a great learning platform for Cloud in itself. At the AWS re:Invent of 2016, I was asked about the resources for learning Cloud, and I said ACG but also mentioned Linux Academy. I had also met the founder of Linux Academy, and we were much alike. We both were trying to grow the same business in the same industry.*"

Right before the pandemic hit in January 2020, the two leading cloud academies decided to join forces for an even more epic journey, and Linux Academy merged with ACG. It required ACG's biggest capital raise to acquire them. Linux Academy excelled at online hands-on labs, so there was a major effort to integrate the best content from both platforms.

"*We all came together under the ACG banner. The friendly feud between our separate user bases disappeared. It was not easy combining the platforms working remotely during the pandemic, but it all worked out. Joining forces meant everyone could benefit from

ACG and Linux Academy's strengths in complementary areas."

Merging the two platforms was like docking two powerful starships - together, their engines could accelerate to new galaxies. With integrated technology and curriculum, A Cloud Guru could slingshot more students to uncharted certification dimensions.

"*It was incredible - investors told us that ACG had more students enrolled than the top six US colleges combined—just mind-blowing growth. We brought cloud skills to millions thanks to our serverless infrastructure that decreased costs. Having an online school during the pandemic was a huge advantage. With traditional classrooms shut down, people couldn't do in-person training or hands-on learning with colleagues. We became the go-to place for cloud learning."*

After acquiring Linux Academy, ACG's main competitor was Pluralsight, the dominant B2B tech skills training player. Ironically, when Ryan first launched his online courses, Pluralsight approached him to become an instructor, and he turned the offer down to build his platform.

Fast forward six years, and ACG came full circle by joining forces with Pluralsight. In 2021, Pluralsight acquired ACG in one of edtech's biggest deals ever. The deal made perfect sense as it blended Pluralsight's broad enterprise reach with ACG's deeper cloud expertise.

"*Pluralsight brought a lot of structure and process to our business and a good recording studio to record courses in Salt Lake City, Utah. ACG had grown too fast and in too many directions, so we inherently needed maturity for further growth. I still work for ACG, but we now operate under Pluralsight. I am a shareholder in Pluralsight and create content for its learners."*

After ACG's acquisition, Ryan finally had more time to relax following eight intense years of hypergrowth. The sale of ACG marked a pivotal point where Ryan could step back from the all-consuming demands of operating a rocket ship startup. Though he is no longer running ACG day-to-day, he still works on updating the video courses. He keeps his tech skills sharp, recently completing a postgraduate diploma in artificial intelligence and machine learning from the University of Texas at Austin.

* * *

Ryan's career journey reveals how self-determination can turn struggle into success. He steered from accounting and immigration law to teaching himself tech skills, ultimately leading to building A Cloud Guru.

While proud of the company's astronomical success, he is ready to enjoy more work-life balance. He beams and asks about his childhood dream of space travel and experiences zero gravity.

"I've had more time to fulfill personal goals, like experiencing zero gravity. I got to do it on a Reduced-gravity aircraft, nicknamed a 'vomit comet' - a plane that flies parabolic loops to create weightlessness. It was an incredible rush floating freely without gravity's pull. Not quite space travel, but I got to live out that childhood dream. And I'm just 41 years old; I may still get to space for real someday, thanks

to the rapid advances in the space travel industry. Who knows what adventure the future holds? For now, I'm enjoying the ride."

ADVICE

Advice when following a Cloud career path

- **Begin with fundamentals** - However dull or time-consuming, you must grasp the fundamentals correctly. Start your cloud journey by understanding the basic building blocks of the Cloud.

- **Dive Deep** - Once you get a foothold, explore where you want to dive. Certifications are not the be-all-and-end-all of the Cloud; there are various streams and verticals within it, so explore it.

- **Plan your learning path** - Plan a focused learning path and achieve a tangible outcome. Track your progress through important milestones and stay away from drifting too much.

ACTION

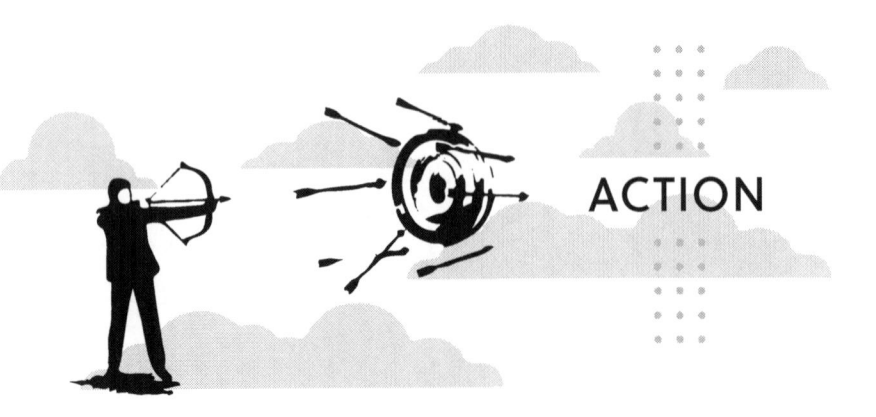

Actions to take that will drive meaningful progress

- **Fix time for consistent learning** - Take time out of your schedule to learn about the Cloud. It could be just an hour during the day, but be consistent with that time.

- **Learn alongside other cloud fanatics** - Learning together is a great way to build social support. If you have a friend or a team on this journey with you, it will surely add value for you.

- **Do practical work** - Don't just learn from a video or an article. Perform the task yourself and practice it to become better at it. Build projects from scratch for the technical know-how.

ALERT

Alerts to avoid common pitfalls that can hinder success

- **Don't quit because of failure** - If you fail any certification or an interview, it's not the end of the road. Don't let that stop you from retaking it. Try again, and eventually, you will pass it by developing a better understanding.

- **Avoid procrastination** - The best time to embark on your career progression journey is now. Procrastination will just add to confusion and delay. Do it now.

- **Not having patience and persistence:** Patience is to be calm no matter what happens, constantly take action to turn it to positive growth opportunities. With patience and persistence the results will start to manifest itself.

Pathfinders   Undefeated   Progressives   Liberators   Accelerators   **Pinnacles**

For J = 1 to AWS

16

Jeff Barr

Vice President and Chief Evangelist, AWS

It's highly unlikely to find someone exploring the Cloud space who hasn't read Jeff's blog posts. If one hasn't, then more likely they are a Cloud spectator than an active player in the Cloud world. But being a spectator is a good starting point too, right?

Was Jeff always an active player, or was he a curious spectator too at first?

Message from the Authors

When we embarked on writing Cloud Career Journeys, a book featuring inspiring stories of people excelling in their Cloud careers, we knew we wanted to include a few well-known personalities from the Cloud industry. At the top of our list was Jeff Barr, Vice President and Chief Evangelist for Amazon Web Services. We thought the chances with somebody as busy and important as Jeff were slim, and he may not have the time to contribute to our book. Nevertheless, we decided to try and reach out.

To our amazement, Jeff graciously made time to meet and hear about our book proposal and the work we do as part of the BeSA (Become a Solutions Architect) program. During the meeting, Jeff remained fully engaged, asking thoughtful questions. When we finished our pitch, he was genuinely excited by our vision for sharing inspiring Cloud journeys. He was so enthusiastic that this *humble* legend offered to write his mini-autobiography for the book. We were thrilled.

Jeff poured tremendous effort and dedicated innumerable hours to writing his story. This is why you will find the book's last story, chronicling Jeff's experience, presented in a completely different format than the others – unfiltered and direct from the source.

We hope you will be as inspired by Jeff Barr's Cloud journey as we were. With his passion and generosity, he truly embodies the spirit of the Cloud community. Presenting to you Jeff's journey to the Cloud, in his own words...

Philadelphia, Pennsylvania

My life began on July 7th, 1960, in Philadelphia, Pennsylvania.

A pair of influences drove my life-long interest in technology. First, my grandfather Benjamin Waldman (or "Pop-Pop" as we called him) was an early adopter. He owned the first black and white TV set in his neighborhood, and my grandmother told stories of how the entire neighborhood would turn out to watch boxing matches. Pop-Pop later earned his living by repairing TVs, back when there were a multitude of vacuum tubes and other replaceable parts inside. Sadly, he passed away before I was five years old. Somehow, in that brief overlap of lives, I was able to gain some of his mechanical aptitude and his enthusiasm for technology.

When I was 3 or 4, my father (who had no mechanical abilities whatsoever) and Pop-Pop were attempting to assemble a play set in our backyard. Both were having trouble figuring out how some of the parts went together, and (per the family stories) I was able to figure out the problem and tell them what to do.

After Pop-Pop was gone, my grandmother kept his toolbox in an apartment closet. For many years, I would open it, and spend time exploring the tools that he left behind. Old electronics components have a certain smell to them, and to this day a whiff of that smell takes me back to those very pleasant times when I had access to Pop-Pop's tools.

The other main influence on me was the United States space program. I had some age-appropriate books that showed pictures of the Mercury and Gemini rockets and promises of the Apollo rockets to come.

Framingham, Massachusetts

I was 6 or 7 when my father got a job in Massachusetts. In preparation for our move, we flew from Pennsylvania to Boston to find a new home. This was my first airplane flight!

My father was in the electronics distribution business, often as the general manager of a branch. These businesses had huge warehouses chock full of electronics parts – resistors, capacitors, test equipment, and much more. By the time I was 11 or 12, I was able to do some order picking in the warehouse – reading the printed order, finding the components, using a ratio scale to get the right quantity, and packing the finished order into a box. I was very curious about all the parts and would always find data sheets to read and study.

In 1969 I remember two important events – the first moon landing, and the debut of the movie **2001: A Space Odyssey.** My 3 younger siblings did not have any interest in the moon landing, and I had to fight for control of the one and only TV. My father took the entire family to the Boston debut of 2001. Everyone else was bored, but I walked out of that movie determined to own a spaceship and a computer.

I was not a good student. I was a good reader and was always asking to be taken to the library, but I never earned top grades. I was the only left-handed student in many classes, and my handwriting left a lot to be desired – I never really learned to write properly, and the sight of a form that must be filled out by hand filled me with dread. The logic and clarity of math always appealed to me, and the concepts always made a lot of sense. However, I rarely ended up with the right answers, and remained frustrated. Many years later, I realized that my exceptionally poor handwriting was probably the root cause here – I often had trouble even reading what I had written, leading to a cascade of errors.

My mother did not have enough patience to have her four children home during the summer and would try to keep us out of the house by enrolling us in camps and other activities. I was not a big fan of outdoors or camping, and when she found a digital logic course at a local high school, I chose that instead. We learned Boolean logic, Karnaugh maps, and spent time creating PC boards and soldering parts onto them.

Massachusetts was home to Digital Equipment Corporation (DEC), and several other minicomputer vendors including Data General and Wang. The junior high school had 3 Teletype devices that were dialed in to the PDP-8 computer at the local high school. Each math class had a 2 week "break" so that we could learn BASIC programming. Despite my long-standing interest in computers, I was very frustrated for the first 9 days, and could not really understand what was going on. My understanding of digital logic was getting in the way here. Each day the teacher would write the same FOR loop on the board, starting with:

```
FOR I = 1 to 10
```

I could imagine some sort of logic that matched these characters and activated some kind of mechanism, but the details were still very unclear. On the last day of class, he wrote a different loop:

```
FOR J = 1 to 20
```

This was the light bulb moment for me. I realized that all of this was somehow parameterized and general purpose, and suddenly everything made a lot more sense. I was now unstoppable and could create programs to do anything that I wanted. In those days, saving a program meant punching it on yellow paper tape at the conclusion of the terminal session, then rolling up the tape and stuffing it into your pocket before rushing to class.

Around this time, I had a job delivering the Boston Herald Traveler newspaper. I would get up at 5 AM, unbundle the stack of papers that had been dropped in front of my house, and then deliver them to 13 or 14 subscribers in my neighborhood. I spent as much time reading the papers as delivering them and became something of a news junkie for a while. I never realized that I was supposed to "sell" additional subscriptions.

Seattle, Washington

My parents' marriage was not very strong, and they would separate and reconnect several times during my teen years. My father's career was rocky as well, and we ended up moving a lot. I started 9th grade in Massachusetts and finished it on Mercer Island, Washington, where I also had a year of high school at a different school. Then we moved to Bellevue, and I had another year of high school there before we moved to Rockville, Maryland for my senior year. All in all that was five schools in four years, a burst of instability that took a long time to stabilize.

While I was in 10th grade my parents signed me up for an event at the Pacific Science Center in Seattle called the Can-Do Workshop, which met for several weekends. At one such event a guy came in and announced that he was forming a "computer club" in Seattle and was looking for others who were interested in the brand-new field of personal computers. I was very interested and was among the first to attend the Northwest Computer Club. This was shortly after the original Altair computer had been launched and excitement was very high. Like Bill Gates and Paul Allen, I had seen the issue of Popular Electronics magazine which announced the Altair. Unlike them, I did not have the business acumen or the technical skills to capitalize on it.

The guy who invited me to the club was named Steve Herber, and we became friends. At some point he told me that he had been hired as the manager of The Retail Computer Store and asked me if I wanted a part-time job as "janitor" so that I could get some access to a computer!

My job was to unpack books, magazines, and marketing materials and put them on the shelves for sale. Being naturally curious, I spent a lot of time reading, and quickly came up to speed in this new and very exciting world of personal computers. As a result, when customers came into the store and had technical questions, the other employees would often send them my way. For all of this, I earned the federally mandated minimum wage, which was somewhere between $2 and $3 per hour.

My time at that store was foundational and therapeutic. Instead of the chaos and instability at home, I had something new, exciting, and positive to focus on. I became better at talking to and working with people of all sorts and learned early on to treat everyone the same. Some of the other store employees went on to work at Microsoft including Mike Courtney, Bob Wallace (who later invented the concept of Shareware), and Tim Paterson (author of MS-DOS). I also got to meet Gary Kildall (author of CP/M), and Philippe Kahn (Borland / Turbo Pascal).

I got to meet Bill Gates, and I showed him how his Altair BASIC interpreter had been illegally incorporated into a computer called CompuColor.

Concurrent with these happy times, I did poorly in high school, once again barely getting by. I have no idea why my parents didn't help with counseling, tutors, or even some encouragement. Looking back this is surprising, given that they were generally very good at encouraging me to explore new things and to develop skills.

With the rise of the personal computer, local and national events began to spring up. In the spring of 1977 the First West Coast Computer Faire was to take place in San Francisco. I was supposed to take my SAT that weekend, but after finding a way to defer it my mother helped me to book a flight and a hotel. I somehow made it from Seattle to the San Francisco airport, and from there to the city. I attended the event, met lots of people, learned a lot, and felt that I was really part of something new and exciting.

Rockville, Maryland

In the summer after 11th grade, we moved to Rockville, Maryland. Before I had even arrived, my father had found a computer store called The Computer Workshop and basically got me a part-time job. I started 12th grade and worked at the store, once again in a new and unfamiliar environment.

Settling in Maryland, my father encouraged me to apply to top-notch colleges, but I didn't. I did not really understand what college was about, I did not know about financial aid, and I was not ready to leave my newfound home. Also, my grades were still awful and I knew that I could not get into MIT, CMU, or similar schools.

I did apply to the University of Maryland and was accepted into their Computer Science program. By this time my father had left for good and even though he promised financial support the details were always fuzzy and I didn't have any confidence that he would follow through.

Towards the end of my senior year in high school, my English teacher took me aside and gave me some life-changing guidance. She basically said that she thought that I had a bright future but that I was not a very good writer. I knew that she was right, and immediately set out to exceed her expectations. Instead of focusing on grammar and on parts of speech (most of which I still find confusing), I invested my time in looking at how good writers used words and punctuation. This was game-changing for me.

Community College

Realizing that my college options were limited, I decided to attend the local community college instead of the University of Maryland. I am not sure what changed, but most of my grades dramatically improved. I was getting A's in all of my computer science classes, as well as in most of the other subjects. Math proved to be the exception, and years of poor results finally caught up with me. I started out by taking Calculus and ended up regressing through 2 or 3 levels of prerequisites before I was ready to climb back up. I passed Calculus, Statistics, and Linear Algebra, and that was enough math for me.

My mother was a secretary at Moshman Associates, a Washington DC consulting company. One day, a senior person was chatting with her and mentioned that he was having trouble hiring programmers. She mentioned my name to him, we chatted, and I was hired as a part-time programmer. I worked on several interesting projects in 6502 assembly language, PL/I, and FORTRAN. The person who hired me was Steve Polyak. He was a great mentor and an equally great friend and advisor.

My suspicions regarding my father's inability to help with college tuition turned out to be true. After just one full-time quarter at community college, he told me that he could no longer help. Wanting to continue, I increased the hours at my programming job. Later that year I decided that I would have to attend college and work full-time concurrently and found a full-time position at a tiny yet impressively named organization called The National Institute for Safety Research, or NISR. In retrospect, I should have negotiated for full-time employment at my previous job, but I didn't know how to start that discussion.

A quarter or two into college, I started to notice a beautiful young woman around campus. She had long dark hair and often wore purple pants (my favorite color). Her friends noticed my interest in her, and we started to study together. Her name was Carmen, she had recently come to the US from Peru, and was also in the computer science program. We did homework together until the end of the school year, and at the end I asked her if I could call her that summer. I did (the next day), we started dating, and we were married in 1982.

Even after leaving The Computer Workshop, I continued to visit their store from time to time. One day they had an extra Apple][for sale at a heavy discount. I bought it, and then took out a loan to buy disk drives, more memory, a modem, and other accessories.

ArpaNet

One day at school, someone handed me a piece of paper with a local phone number on it. They told me "call this number with a modem" and I did. I am sure that they already knew that I had a computer and as modem, both rare to have at home at that time. When I made the call it answered "PENTAGON TIP". This, it turns out, was a dial-up connection to the ArpaNet. After some experimentation I found that I could connect to any of the hosts by typing "C" and a number from 1 to 255. The host would answer with a Unix login, and I could login with username and password "guest."

As part of my investment in my Apple][, I bought a then-new game called Zork. I spent a while playing it, and then attempted to create a complete map on a large piece of posterboard. I made great progress and was sure that I was nearly done, and then entered a new phase of the game which unveiled a multitude of new rooms and passageways. With limited time, I gave up on my effort.

I continued my quest to be current and well-informed about the state of the personal computer industry, tracking new chips, new computers, and new software as diligently as possible. I bought a book on the Motorola 68000 (one of the first true 32-bit processors), and learned its architecture in detail. I was also aware of Intel's chips including the 8-bit 8080 and the 16-bit 8086.

As the personal industry grew, rumors of IBM's imminent entry spread. They made their big announcement and everyone was eager to get a look at their offering. I would sometimes visit my local ComputerLand (part of a national chain of computer stores), and they were soon to be among the first to get a floor model of the brand-new IBM PC.

I went over to my local store at my first opportunity, and peered intently at the exposed motherboard and processor. Another curious person asked me what I thought about it, and we started chatting. His name was Dave Dikel, and I told him that I thought that the Motorola 68000 was a much more interesting and powerful processor. He raised an eyebrow and told me that he was working for a company that was building a computer around the 68000. We exchanged contact info, and I was eager to learn more.

Intellimac

A week or so later we touched base and I visited his office nearby. The company was called Intellimac and they had promised to build a multiuser computer that would be host to an Ada compiler from a company called Telesoft. The president of Intellimac was a charismatic leader by the name of Dick Naedel. After our interview he offered me a job as a "Systems Programmer" at an hourly rate of $15 per hour.

I resigned from Moshman Associates (perhaps not as gracefully as I should have), and started my new full-time job at Intellimac in very early 1982. During the interview, Dick told me that the operating system (Telesoft ROS) was already running in single-user mode, and that my job was to make it run in multi-user mode. I was not totally sure that I could actually do that, but I had a lot of confidence in my ability to do crazy and nearly impossible things with code. On my first day I found that ROS could not even run on the Intellimac hardware. Undaunted, I had a three month timeline to go from that point to a fully running multi-user system. I started by writing device drivers for the floppy disk and the hard drive, and within 6 weeks I had ROS running and stable. With 1.5 months left to go, the next was to host 4 copies of the same operating system in carefully partitioned memory, and to coordinate shared access to peripherals. This sounds impossible but it was actually fairly straightforward and I made it all work. Intellimac was able to deliver multiple 4-user Ada systems to commercial and military customers at a very economical per-user price. Encouraged by what I was able to do in a short time and with very limited resources, the company started to promise customers that they could run Unix and the ROS operating system side-by-side. They did this without my knowledge or consent, and I had no idea how to do this.

Carmen and I were married in August of 1982, and we recently celebrated our 41st wedding anniversary. Finances were very tight at that point, and we both worked hard to build solid foundations for our future.

At some point along the way, my friend Steve Herber sent me a thick manual that encompassed all of the documentation for BSD Unix. True to my nature, I spent a lot of time reading this documentation and learning about different flavors of Unix.

Contel Information Systems

My next job was with Contel Information Systems in Bethesda, Maryland where I was able to work with my good friend Steve Polyak once again. The company had landed a contract with the now-defunct American Stock Exchange to automate various aspects of their trading floor. This part of the company was a division of Continental Telecom, then a phone company of some sort. Contel built a broadband network for the stock exchange (this was before Ethernet became ubiquitous) that used equipment and cabling originally designed for closed-circuit television. Contel designed and fabricated the network controller, which was known as a Bus Interface Unit, or BIU. For reasons that were never revealed to me, they built exactly 100 of these boards, some reasonable fraction (say 70%) or so actually worked as expected. Before I arrived, they had decided on a one-to-one mapping between BIUs and some small printers which resided on the trading floor. Due to the shortage of BIUs they decided that each one could drive four printers, and they asked me to make this happen. The printers spoke a low-level networking protocol known as X.25, with drivers written in a combination of Z-80 assembly language and C. I studied the code and figured out how to multiplex four printers, which turned out to be reasonably straightforward. Debugging was another matter entirely. We did not have a complete test environment in Maryland. After I had code that seemed to work in my limited local environment, I would "burn" it onto EPROM Erasable Programmable Read-Only Memory) chips and fly to New York to do testing and debugging in-situ. For several weeks I was able to do multiple, one-day round trips between Washington, DC and New York each week. This was before airport security became a big deal, and it was possible to simply walk on to a shuttle flight without a reservation, pay on-board, and fly! I was able to get the printers and the code up and running, and the project was a big success. I also did several other Unix-related projects while I was at Contel, using the knowledge that I had gained from reading and re-reading the BSD Unix documentation.

American University

During my time at Contel I finally did the paperwork to graduate from Montgomery Community College, and applied to the part-time Computer Science program at nearby American University. I was fortunate that Contel had a tuition reimbursement program that would allow me to take up to two work-related courses per semester. I took full advantage of this, and took every undergraduate and graduate CS program that American University had to offer. I did all of this while working full time, and even while traveling back and forth to New York. Having a lot of stamina and the ability to handle work, school, and family simultaneously were all big success factors.

Our son Stephen was born in 1985 with four more children to follow over the next 10 years.

We also bought our first home while I was at Contel, with a down payment of $5,000 and a mortgage of close to $100,000. My parents advised us against this, but the house turned out to be a great investment, more than doubling in price over the time that we owned it.

American Management Systems

I was getting a bit restless, and at that point most of the interesting tech stuff was happening in Silicon Valley. We were very attached to our respective families in Maryland and a move to Silicon Valley was out of the question at that point. I started to look for a new and more exciting job, and soon found one at American Management Systems (AMS). The person who interviewed me (let's call him JW) was forming a new group to build and sell Unix applications and hired me as a senior developer. I wrote an application called Directory Shell, which was a terminal-oriented interface to Unix. I wrote tens of thousands of lines of C code and the first version was very functional and polished. JW had a deep disdain for marketing, and insisted that high-quality applications could somehow sell themselves. This was not true then and it is not true today, but he had an Ivy League MBA and I thought that he knew what he was doing. JW had a fierce, argumentative personality and often clashed with many of the people around him. At some point he would inevitably "turn" on those around him, lash out, and create ill will.

The lure of the West Coast was still there and on a whim I accepted an invitation to interview at Microsoft in 1998. The cash part of the offer was almost insultingly low, but there were plenty of stock options attached. When I told JW that I was leaving, he convinced AMS to double my cash salary, and we had to say no to Microsoft. This decision cost me hundreds of millions of dollars that would have been mine had I retained all of the stock from the initial offer.

Visix Software

JW engineered a spin-out of our group into a new, venture-funded startup known as Visix Software. Headquartered in Reston, Virginia the company grew to nearly 200 employees at peak. I was VP of Engineering, and we produced two main products under my lead. Looking Glass was a visual, graphical interface to Unix, and Galaxy was a cross-platform application environment. Both were packed-full of features. We signed many contracts with hardware vendors, getting them to ship Looking Glass on their Unix workstations. True to form, the company did not have a VP of Marketing, with JW still convinced that features would make products sell better. In frustration at our limited success, I began to seek speaking slots at conferences. JW did not see the value in this as a marketing tool, and disparagingly called me "The world's highest paid presales guy." He was beginning to turn against me, but the shares that I had been granted in Visix made me overstay my welcome. There was a very concrete plan to go public, which never actually came to pass.

Vertex Development

I was tired of Visix and left in 1995 to create Vertex Development, my consulting identity. My first customer was named Caldera, and they were working to create a user-friendly desktop version of Linux. They purchased a license to the Visix Looking Glass product and my first project was to port it to Linux, version 1-something. I was also asked to reduce the memory footprint, and spent some time building a very cool dynamic loading system. I made everything work as planned, and Caldera was a great customer. I did not tell Carmen at the time I left Visix that the success of my first project (and the ability to feed our five young & hungry children) was dependent on a then-new operating system that I had never actually used before! That project led to another, and I spent over two years doing many different types of programming, marketing, and writing projects.

Microsoft

In mid-1997 Microsoft called me again and this time we decided to make the move from Maryland to Washington! The company did its best to make our move smooth and easy, setting us up with a fully furnished temporary house, two rental cars, and generous allowances for personal expenses. After years of preparation, I was finally going to hit the big time and work at a name-brand company. I was hired on to the team that was building Visual Basic as a development manager. My first assignment was to take a piece of code called the DHTML Page Designer and fix (to quote the General Manager) the few remaining bugs. It turned out that the code had been written in a huge hurry by a creative developer who was very good at implementing the essentials and leaving a lot of loose ends behind for later. Before I even figured this out, I realized that Microsoft was not all that I had expected. Within 3 weeks I realized that the team moved very slowly and that releasing VB6 would be a long and painful slog. We finally shipped VB6 after a long, tedious development period. The DHTML Page Designer used an embedded part of Internet Explorer as an editing surface. It turned out that the VB team was the only internal or external client for this surface (code named Trident) and it was hard to get the IE team to fix bugs or to add features. In particular, the VB editing model supported the ability to shift-select multiple objects and to operate on them as a group. Trident did not support this and the team was not inclined to support it. Having spent a lot of time debugging obscure bugs within Trident, I had a unique outsider's view of the architecture and the code and decided to implement multiple selections myself. I did this without the consent of my own management and without telling the IE team, even though we met with them on a weekly basis. This work took me several weeks, and when it was working properly I brought the finished work to the next weekly meeting. The IE team was amazed at my work, and accepted it as an external check-in to their code base. Even though I had pulled off to me what was a major accomplishment, VB management was not happy that I had gone rogue and done this on my own. It was the right thing to do, and I am still happy that I did it. During the VB6 development cycle, one of the devs on my team discovered some fairly serious security issues that involved IE and Windows Millennium. Following protocol, we filed a bug, which was closed as won't-fix. Upset with this decision, I escalated to the GM and, with my team, we walked across campus to press for a reversal. Sadly he said "Even if we fix this one bug, there are likely more, so this won't make a difference." To this day, I remember walking back across campus with my team, realizing that we were not proud to be Microsoft employees that day.

After we shipped VB6, I interviewed for, and became, a Program Manager (PM), responsible for designing web services features for the next version of Visual Studio, then code-named Project Phoenix. Instead of writing code I wrote specs, and worked with the dev teams to get them implemented.

When I joined Microsoft I committed to working there for 3 years. As that time approached I realized that little had happened to reverse my initial disillusionment, and that I was ready for another change. The Internet was beginning to be a big deal, dot-com companies were springing up out of nowhere, and I wanted to be where the action was.

XML, RSS, Headline Viewer, Syndic8

During my time at Microsoft, XML was invented, as was RSS and the concept of syndicated news. Wanting to make use of RSS and to learn how to build real apps using VB6, I wrote a little app that I called Headline Viewer, and gave it away for free. I collected RSS feeds from lots of sites, and encouraged other sites to generate and share their feeds. This was a very successful side project and I got a lot of positive feedback. At one point the RSS community encouraged me to separate the app and the list of feeds, and to come up with a way to allow others to find, validate, and share them. I was ready to build a serious web app, and learned PHP + MySQL in order to do so. I registered the domain Syndic8.com (short for "syndicate") and eventually wrote tens of thousands of lines of PHP. The database schema was very complex, with around 50 or 60 tables. I sold ads and links, and had a very nice side business going for a while. The site was hosted at a colo facility, where I rented a Linux server for several hundred dollars per month. Syndic8 included a comprehensive web API using the then-prominent XML-RPC protocol. Little did I know that this site and this API would open the door to my future job at Amazon. The site remained active several years into my employment with Amazon. The site was slow and perpetually overloaded, and I spent far too much time studying MySQL slow query logs and fine-tuning my database. Today, it would be so much easier to host the site on a small fleet of EC2 instances and to use Amazon Aurora for my database needs.

Consulting Once More

One of my friends had built and sold a startup and had become a venture capitalist. When I was looking for something to do should I leave Microsoft, he proposed that I could do technical due diligence for him, investigating startups as potential investments for him. I reactivated my consulting company and dove right in. I would talk to the engineers at the startup, look at their code and their architecture, and make recommendations. Several recommendations resulted in funding and my friend gave me the opportunity to be a Consulting VP of Engineering or Consulting CTO to several of the startups, which was fun. A lot of my projects were related to web services in some way – SOAP, XSLT, WSDL, and so forth.

This was around 2000 / 2001, when most of the web services were technically oriented and not conducive to demos: stock quotes, currency conversions, and so forth. I regularly showed technical folks how a client could connect to a service across the internet, retrieve some data, and display it. They were in the best position to appreciate how amazing and how powerful this was (for the time). Business folks, especially VCs, were a much harder sell. They did not appreciate what I showed them, and were not generally interested in funding the development of tools that would make it easier to build and/or call these simple, somewhat dry services.

The First Amazon Web Service

In the spring of 2002 I became aware of the very first Amazon web service. I was very active in the web services community at the time, and believe that I learned of this service hours after it launched. I signed up for the beta, downloaded the SDK, printed the 30-something page manual, and dove right in. I built a PHP wrapper around the raw SOAP APIs and called it PIA – PHP Interface to Amazon. It used to be hosted on SourceForge, but I can no longer find a trace of it. I also captured all of my feedback and emailed it to the contact-us address in the documentation, expecting it to disappear into the void. To my surprise, an Amazon product manager named Bill Bazley replied to my message and invited me to Amazon HQ for further discussion. I drove from the suburbs into the city and met Bill at the now-legendary Pac-Med (Pacific Medical) building in Beacon Hill.

A month or two later Bill's colleague Sarah Spillman invited me to attend a little developer conference that Amazon was planning to host. I accepted, and made my way to Pac-Med once again. I can still remember being in one of the upper-floor conference rooms for the day, along with 4 or 5 other early web services developers. We sat in the center of the somewhat circular room, with a dozen or two Amazonians sitting at the periphery. The speakers gave us an update on what had taken place after the beta announcement – developers (like me) quickly found the offering, gave it a try, and were deploying finished applications within 48 hours. As has often been shared, this was one hint to Amazon that they could successfully build and market services for developers. At one point, a speaker (he or she, I wish could remember) said something to the effect of "We are so impressed with what has happened so far, we plan to find and share additional services." This was the light-bulb moment for me. My time at Microsoft had given me an appreciation for the value of APIs and developer communities, and I quickly saw what the future could be. I went and found Sarah, and told her that I wanted to be a part of "this", even though I was not quite sure what "this" was. She told me that she could help to make that happen, and before long I was booked for an interview loop!

I was booked for an interview as a development manager. I had been an Amazon customer since October 1996, when I bought a book called PC Roadkill, but knew little about the business or technical structure of the company. During my full-day interview I was asked to write several string processing routines and a SQL query or two. I also being asked if I knew what Amazon did, and if I had ever made a purchase. The interview apparently went well and I was offered a position as a Development Manager on the Amazon Associates team, reporting to Larry Hughes. We were just about to leave for a family vacation in Cabo san Lucas, and I accepted the offer while we were there.

Joining Amazon

We returned from vacation and I wrapped up a few remaining consulting projects, then reported for work in mid-August of 2002. My initial assignment was to take ownership of a set of Perl scripts that were used to generate daily reports for the members of the

Amazon Associates program. The scripts were fairly fragile and we were regularly paged in the middle of the night to fix issues. The scripts had to run to completion within 24 hours so as to not overlap with the next run, which was a cause for anxiety.

In early September I was asked to brief some of the leaders on web services as part of a "chalk talk," and prepared a 26-slide presentation.

During one of my first 1-on-1's with Larry, he said "I know that you really came here to work on web services, so use some of your time to help out the team." This was, looking back, one of those fortuitous forks in the road that led me to where I am today. The initial web service was still in beta. I answered questions on the user forums, built a simple set of monitors to ensure that the service endpoints were working as expected, and even implemented another type of search. The early success that had led to that initial developer conference continued, and more outside developers signed up each and every day. One fateful day, several members of the development team (including the leader, Rob Frederick) showed up at my desk unannounced. In a somewhat ominous tone they told me "You are the new guy, so we are dumping this conference speaking slot on you," with the expectation that I would be unhappy. To their surprise I was happy to accept it, and gave my first-ever talk in early 2003. It went well and before too long other requests started to come in.

At some point in early 2003, Larry and Sarah came to me and said "We have an open position called Web Services Evangelist. We've been looking externally to fill it, but you are already doing most of what we want. Would you like to take this role?" This was yet another fork in the road, and one that I was eager to accept. After checking in with my family to make sure that they would be OK with the amount of travel that this would entail, I accepted. That year I made trips to Japan, the UK, and many US cities to talk about web services. I was non-discriminatory and would happily show up at any audience comprised of developers.

With the success of this first service, the company was ready to build more. Along with a few other Amazonians, I was invited to spend a day (or was it a half day) at Jeff Bezos' boathouse where we would brainstorm about ideas for future web services. I did not realize just how much of a pivotal moment in time this would prove to be, and did not take notes or pictures to memorialize it.

In 2004 Andy Jassy was famously asked to build a web services business and I was fortunate to be able to sit just one office away from him. Andy didn't know a lot about developers when he started, and I was able to answer all of his questions and to provide him with insights into this important new customer set. I was also privileged to be able to read and to supply him with feedback on his now-famous narrative that was used to define what is now the AWS business. Andy's narrative used the list developed at the boathouse as source material, further refining and proposing construction of multiple services. I was already very busy with the small portfolio of pre-AWS services that existed at that point, and was worried about my ability to further scale. At one point I wrote a paper that outlined the entire concept of developer relations and shared it with Andy. One crucial element was a blog, and after a lot of discussion I launched what is now the AWS News Blog in November of 2004 with a simple "Welcome" post. In what is now a clear theme here and in my life in general, I did not know just how important that step forward would prove to be.

For years, my main duties as Web Services Evangelist consisted of delivering in-person talks, writing blog posts, and sharing them on social media. I also built and tried to run a small team of evangelists, but after struggling as a manager for several years I was able to revert to being an individual contributor. There was very little in way of process in the early days. I would receive a heads-up on a pending launch via email, along with documentation and some technical details. Over time, starting with the 2016 hiring of Ana Visneski, the process became more structured and robust.

The early informality on the blog gave me a lot of flexibility to innovate and to put my personal touch on every post. Before the first post was even published, I worked with Amazon PR to lay down some guidelines that would allow me to sidestep the usual review from PR and Legal. It was clear from the beginning that the blog was a special case, and I am happy that they were able to create a set of rules that kept the bureaucracy to a minimum.

University of Washington / MCDM

In 2008 or 2009 I was asked to be an adviser to the Masters of Communication in Digital Media (MCDM) program at the University of Washington. After reviewing the courses for several quarters, I asked the director if I could drop in on the classes from time to time. Minutes later, I asked if I could apply to the program instead, and of course he agreed.

In the fall of 2010 I became a graduate student while still keeping up with all of my AWS duties. This sometimes became tricky due to travel, but it was thoroughly enjoyable and I am more than happy that I did it.

In the spring of 2013 I was ready to graduate, and proposed an AWS Road Trip as an independent study project. It was accepted, and my final semester was consumed with planning and execution.

The Public Wiki

From the beginning I wanted to make each of my trips as worthwhile as possible. In addition to delivering a presentation at an industry event or a user group, I would seek out other opportunities to meet with developers, web services users, and AWS customers. In order to simplify and scale this process, I created an open scheduling system using a publicly accessible wiki in 2006 or 2007. As part of my preparation for a trip to a particular city, I would create a new page on the wiki and share it on social media. Interested parties would find the page, locate and claim an open time, and enter their contact information. In addition to allowing me to make great use of my time, I was able to meet lots people that I would not have known to contact.

Several times, people took the time to clean up my calendar, going so far as to rearrange meetings in order to reduce my travel time. Or, they realized that I was meeting with someone they knew, and would arrange a combined meeting. One time, a mysterious entry appeared: "Four guys from the FBI need to meet with you, details in email." We arranged to have dinner at a steakhouse in Washington, DC. It turned out that they all wanted to work for AWS, and I made that happen. One of those people is now the CSO of Amazon, another the CSO of AWS, another is a Distinguished Engineer / VP, and the fourth had a productive career at AWS before moving on.

As AWS grew, I eventually had to abandon the wiki due to security concerns, but it remains one of favorite innovations.

AWS Road Trip 2013

For several years I had wanted to find a way to visit multiple developer user groups in quick succession. For my independent study project I mapped out a set cities that I wanted to visit as part of a drive across the US, then announced the trip in a blog post. Within hours I had commitments from user groups in 14 cities and the trip was on! After a lot of planning, I set out in May 2013 and over the course of three weeks I drove 5,550 miles and spoke to user groups in all 14 of those cities. This was one of my favorite activities as Chief

Evangelist; from time to time I still meet people who attended one of my talks.

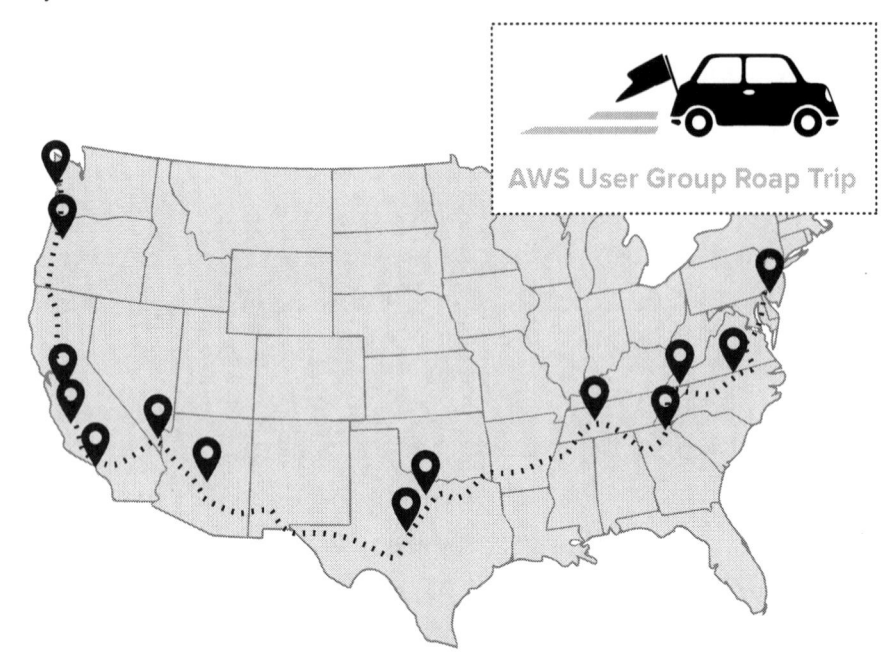

AWS User Group Roap Trip

Hit the road, Jeff!

Purple Hair

Purple has always been my favorite color. In early 2017 I was looking for an excuse or opportunity to dye my hair and one Friday I found it. I had been asking the Amazon WorkSpaces team to give me access to a pre-release "bundle" that would allow me to have even more memory and processing power. As an incentive I told them that I would gladly dye my hair purple if they were able to deliver by my deadline. They did, and I did, and my purple hair became a trademark of sorts. I have shown up for re:Invent with fresh, bright purple several times and it is always a great conversation starter.

Over the Years

I have been lucky enough to be the first (or among the first) to take on many different assignments as part of my role as Chief Evangelist for AWS. In addition to what I have already mentioned, I was the first AWS person to visit and speak in London, Tokyo, and Beijing. In the beginning there were no local offices or support staff, so I was very much on my own.

Today, at age 63 and after more than 21 years at Amazon, I am just a few years away from retirement. I have written and published approximately 3300 blog posts over the years, and continue to produce them at a steady pace. I am also spending time reviewing and commenting on the work of the other members of the AWS News Blog team, with the expectation that I will be able to step away from the blog in November 2024, when it will be 20 years old. Little did I know when I started the blog back in 2004 that it would become the work that defined and perhaps capped my career. While I am proud of the sheer volume of content that I have created, what really gives me satisfaction is to meet some of the people that have read and benefitted from it over the years. There's something very special about knowing that my own efforts to learn and share have helped so many others to gain some knowledge and then used it to make progress.

I enjoy mentoring, and have an active roster of mentees, many in the early to middle stages of their respective careers. Again, like blogging, it is satisfying to my small contribution amplified and applied by others to their benefit.

While I have firm plans to retire from active blogging in November 2024, I am still charting a course for the last couple of years on the job. I have lots of ideas, some plans, and you have definitely not heard (or seen) the last of me!

Advice when following a Cloud career path

- **Take the fork in the road** - When you are presented with a new career opportunity that takes you by surprise, take it. Many times, others can see ways for you to apply your experience and skills in new and interesting ways.

- **Be an early adopter** - Be among the first to recognize, experiment with, and comment on new applications, tools, devices, processes, and platforms. Recognize that not all of them will succeed, but be prepared in case they do.

- **Get double value** - After you have invested time in learning something new, create and share some content that documents and summarizes your learning journey. This is a "cheat code" that lets you do something once and get value from it twice.

ACTION

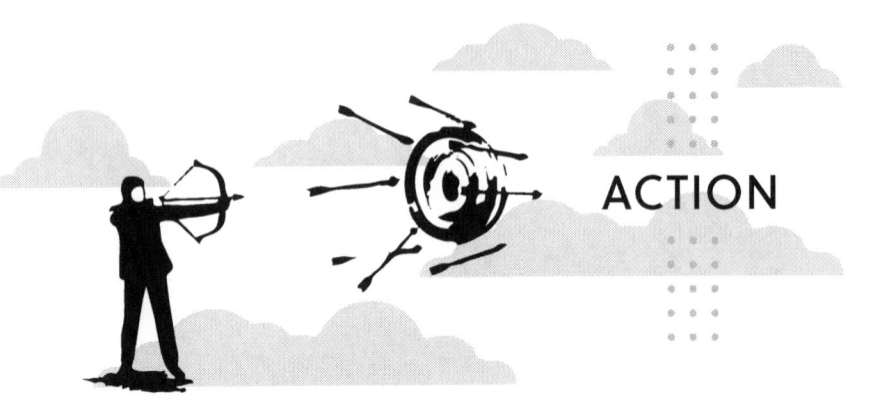

Actions to take that will drive meaningful progress

- **Schedule time for learning** - Don't leave learning to chance or for when you have nothing else to do. Find a time on your calendar (at least monthly, but preferably weekly) and block it off as learning time.

- **Be on the lookout** - Arrange for information on topics that are of interest and value to you to simply show up. Use alerts, periodic searches, RSS feeds, newsletters, and other subscriptions to your advantage.

- **Welcome newcomers** - Make sure that newcomers feel welcome in the meetings, groups, neighborhoods, and communities that you curate and participate in.

ALERT

Alerts to avoid common pitfalls that can hinder success

- **Beware of friction & tax** - Everything that you own, and each relationship that you have, requires time, attention, money, and other resources to keep them healthy. Choose possessions and relationships with care, keep them healthy, and don't let them own you.

- **Don't get stuck in the past** - Respect the past, but embrace the future, especially when it comes to technology. Every piece of tech was once new, amazing, and all-powerful. Let it have its day as the best and brightest, then embrace the future and let the past move on.

- **Watch for fakes and conspiracy theories** - There's never been more of either, and the purveyors are increasingly sophisticated. Don't be fooled!

Free Resources | 371

Now it's your turn to
chart your unique
Cloud Career Journey

**Claim your free resources from
our sponsors to get started**

Platinum Sponsors

WHIZLABS

PLURALSIGHT

DigitalCloud TRAINING

TD TUTORIALS DOJO

Plan your Cloud Career Journey with these exclusive free resources

https://bit.ly/ccj-free

Scan QR code to get free resources from:

Whizlabs

Pluralsight

Digital Cloud Training

Tutorials Dojo

Accelerate your Cloud Career Journey

with

WHIZLABS

Get a FREE one-month Whizlabs Premium+ Subscription worth $29 with each book purchase

Sharpen your skills with experimental learning through Hands-on Labs, Sandbox, Video Courses and Practice Exams

www.whizlabs.com

Build real-world cloud skills to unlock exciting opportunities in the Cloud with

DigitalCloud TRAINING

Enjoy 30 Days of Free Access to Digital Cloud Training's Learning Platform

Over 150 Hours of AWS Video Training and 3,000+ AWS Practice Questions (worth $19.99)

www.digitalcloud.training

PLURALSIGHT

The journey to cloud mastery begins with a single skill

Build cloud skills from industry experts. Then learn by doing with hands-on labs and sandboxes so you can tackle your next project or career change with confidence.

Get a FREE one-month Pluralsight Skills Premium subscription worth $45

Your one-stop learning portal for AWS certification and other Cloud topics

TUTORIALS DOJO

Kick-start your Cloud Career Journey with a FREE AWS Certified Cloud Practitioner video course with 1 full practice exam and tens of PlayCloud AWS Hands-On Labs (worth $9.99)

https://tutorialsdojo.com/

AWS Skill Builder

Advance your professional goals, prepare for an AWS Certification exam, and dive deep to gain the knowledge and skills necessary to innovate.

Building and innovating - it all starts with a Skill Builder subscription. Unlock 1,000+ lab experiences in a safe, no-fee sandbox environment, and more!

Unlock your 7-day free trial at skillbuilder.aws

aws training and certification

topmate

If you are a mentor

Start you Side Hustle Today

Turn your passion and knowledge into a thriving business. Help your audience get ahead in life

Need a mentor?

Find them on Topmate.io

Boost your career to new heights

with the exclusive

Cloud Career Journeys - Starter Kit

https://bit.ly/CCJ-StarterKit

The Starter Kit equips you with tools and resources to transform and advance your career within 6 to 12 months.

Starter Kit includes following:

- 6 months Whizlabs Premium+ Access worth $100
- 6 months Pluralsight Premium Access worth $200
- 12 months Free Access to the AWS Cloud Practitioner Ultimate Training Package from Digital Cloud Training (worth $39.99)
- Access to exclusive community and monthly group sessions by experts on career guidance
- Roadmaps for following cloud roles
    - Cloud Devops engineer by Nana Janashia (Founder, TechWorld with Nana)
    - Cloud Solutions Architect by Jon Bonso (Founder, Tutorials Dojo)
    - Platform engineer by Mumshad Mannambeth (Founder, KodeKloud)
    - Cloud Security engineer by Ian Austin (Founder, PwnedLabs.io)
    - Cloud Developer by Sandeep Das (AWS Hero)
    - Cloud AI/Ml Engineer by Kesha Williams (AWS Hero)
- $100 discount on Digital Cloud Training's Cloud Mastery Bootcamp
- 30% off on all Video courses and Practice Tests on Tutorials Dojo
- 50% off on KodeKloud Pro Subscriptions
- 15% discount on all bootcamps and courses of TechWorld with Nana
- 20% discount (max $100) for 5 mentoring sessions on topmate.io

- 20% off on all resume services packages by GetSetResumes.com
- 50% off on the monthly plan for AI Resume builder (resumod.io)
- 20% off on all Linux Foundation Certifications for Kubernetes (via KodeKloud)

Achieve your goals faster with Cloud Career Journeys - Starter Kit

Scan QR code to get started

https://bit.ly/CCJ-StarterKit

BeSA
Become a Solutions Architect

This is a unique opportunity for you to be mentored by experts to acquire skills to become a Solutions Architect.

In this free program, we focus on technical and behavioural concepts for becoming a successful Solutions Architect, help you upskill for certifications, and provide interview preparation support.

Check more details here:

https://www.youtube.com/@be-SA

A team of experts will guide you to your next career step.

Your reviews mean a lot to us.

If the book resonated with you,
please leave a review on Amazon

Want to collaborate or bulk order the book?

Send an email to

info@cloudcareerjourneys.com

Printed by Amazon Italia Logistica S.r.l.
Torrazza Piemonte (TO), Italy